MY SILENT SCREAM

Finding Hope & Grace to Endure

Inside a mother's struggle to raise a child
with OCD, ADHD, & Asperger's Syndrome

By
Dee Phillips-Goodnight

My Silent Scream:
Finding Hope & Grace to Endure
Inside a mother's struggle to raise a child with
OCD, ADHD, & Asperger's Syndrome
ISBN: 978-1-936314-54-6

Copyright © 2011 by Dee Phillips-Goodnight
www.mysilentscream.org

Published by Word and Spirit Books
P.O. Box 701403
Tulsa, Oklahoma 74170

"Mom?"

"Yes, Ross."

*"I'm just not, you know, as easy as other kids.
Am I, Mom?"*

FOREWORD

Nobody knows a child better than his mother. A mother just has that God-given innate sixth-sense which tells her when something is wrong with her child. Many times I've witnessed mothers consoling crying babies with the words, "Mommy knows, Mommy knows." Mothers know when something is "not quite right" physically and mentally with their child.

Dads may notice as well when something is "psychologically off" with their child, but they rarely have that sixth-sense type of intuition. It's actually not unusual for a father to be oblivious to his children's thoughts and feelings. An old saying in psychiatry is that if Mom and Dad disagree on what's happening with their child, the mom will be right at least 100% of the time. While this is not meant to be taken literally, it does emphasize the superior insight of mothers.

Moms are also committed to do whatever it takes in finding out what's wrong with the mental state of their son or daughter and then getting them the help they need. Dads don't always want to know. I'm certainly not trying to beat up on fathers—nor question their love and devotion to their offspring. But many times I've heard men attempt to explain away their son's unacceptable behaviors by statements such as "well he's all boy" or "he's just a little rambunctious."

It's not uncommon for fathers to resist searching for psychological help for their child for the following reasons:

1. I don't want people knowing (or asking questions) about what goes on privately in our family.

2. If my child thinks there is something mentally wrong with him it could damage his self-esteem.

3. My child will be labeled by others now (especially the school).

4. If there's something wrong with my child, that's a failure on my part as a father.

Much of this resistance deals with concern of how others will perceive the family rather than confronting the specific psychological challenges facing a child. Mothers can get caught up in this as well. And in parents' defense, there is some truth to these four statements—a huge stigma still surrounds mental health in this country. And parents are often the first who are blamed when their child has problems.

The overwhelming majority of mothers that I've dealt with in my practice as a psychiatrist are willing to do whatever it takes to find help for their child—no matter the price. And I'm not talking money here, but personal sacrifice. A mother will abandon her dreams, well being, and security in life for her child if needed.

We've seen shows and read books about women trapped in Middle Eastern countries who risked their own lives in order to enable their children to escape and lead a better life. I know a mother who drove her daughter six hours every Friday to Houston to get the cancer treatment she needed on Saturday—then drove back on Sunday. On top of this, that mother worked a full time job Monday through Thursday.

Dee's story about her son Ross is a perfect example of a mother's instinct and insight. Dee's unfathomable love for Ross and her unshakable faith in God propelled her onward to find answers.

My Silent Scream is a rollercoaster ride of a family's trying, tragedy, and triumph. You'll fall in love with Ross as you discover the wonderful heart and charisma of this young man; though there will be times that you'll feel like sending him to his room and telling him not to come out until he's twenty-one. *My Silent Scream* is also a story of high expectations, hard work, and hope. Most of all, it's the journey of a mother struggling to raise a son who's "not quite right" in today's world. On this journey she discovers the real meaning of God's strength and blessing.

I consider myself among one of the privileged few because God has allowed me to play a small role in Ross and Dee's lives. Their story continues to remind me that life is not always what we expect nor originally hope for, but no matter what circumstance we find ourselves in—magnificently splendid or utterly horrible—<u>God is with us</u>—whether we realize it or not—He's providing for us; all of the time.

Todd Clements M.D.
February 2011

INTRODUCTION

"Adversity causes some men to break; others to break records."

—William A. Ward

Therefore, since we have been justified through faith, we have peace with God through our Lord Jesus Christ, through whom we have gained access by faith into this grace in which we now stand. And we rejoice in the hope of the glory of God. Not only so, but we also rejoice in our suffering, because we know suffering produces perseverance; perseverance, character; and character hope. And hope does not disappoint us, because God has poured out his love into our hearts by the Holy Spirit, whom he has given us.

Romans 5: 1-5

This book is a raw look inside our daily lives. As I look back over the years since Ross was born, my life has been one big puzzle. Some pieces fit together; while in other areas, I'm still trying to bring the pieces together to make sense. Everyday, I strive to find one more piece that fits to make the puzzle recognizable, to be able to understand the total picture. My goal is to share with you the way Ross expresses himself and how the characteristics of his disorders manifest themselves in our everyday life. Perhaps I will describe an account along the journey of our lives that may be similar to what you are facing with your own child. I hope to bring validation to you as you read this book. I hope to make you smile, and above all, give you hope.

I want to encourage you to keep pressing forward and never give up! As I begin, I pray that my words and the recounting of my experience will be a blessing to those who read them and will, in some way through God's grace, present each individual with something that can be useful in their situation.

Fall 2008

The room was dark, it was still daytime, but I had closed all the blinds. I knelt beside the bed and sobbed. It was hard for me to get a deep breath. My body ached and my heart felt broken. Visions and voices played over and over in my head. I had just finished meeting with Ross's teachers...all of them. I could tell by their facial expressions when I entered the room, that it wasn't going to be a pleasant meeting. The air in the room was heavy. There were times I tilted my head back, just to get a deep breath of air.

As I sat there listening to each teacher describe Ross's behaviors, I felt weak. It was like someone stuck a needle in me and deflated my strength. Some of the teachers seemed compassionate and others, highly frustrated. I kept wishing the words they were using to describe my child weren't true, but I knew the sad reality all too well myself. One teacher commented that she had over 25 students in her class, and she simply didn't have the time or energy to give that Ross demanded.

- "He's argumentative."

- "He can't keep up in class."

- "I can't get him to do his schoolwork."

- "He just wants to go to the library and read non-fiction books."

- "He's obsessed with building a spaceship."

- "He's paranoid to go outside."

- "He's not in touch with reality."

- "Dee, I think he's close to a breakdown."

We all agreed that something needed to be done, but exactly what that "something" was, was always the question. If I knew what to do, I would already be doing it! Ross seemed to be growing increasingly agitated and was "melting down" in class frequently.

Ross was not only struggling at school, but things at home were on the decline as well. He now had added a list of phobias to the mix of issues we were already confronting. In addition to the traditional Asperger's characteristics, Ross was now experiencing unrealistic fears. He did not want to walk from the car in the garage to the house for fear that a wasp might attack him. He didn't want to take a shower without me standing right next to the shower door. He thought a dinosaur might come through the wall or hot lava might spew from the faucet. He refused to walk upstairs without someone with him. He became hypersensitive of crossing bridges while riding in the car. He wanted his window in his bedroom concreted shut so that no "predators" could enter. He especially was concerned about cougars. If the heater in the house came on, he jumped as if he were on edge. He refused to walk from the bus stop to our house. He would literally go door to door to find someone in the neighborhood who would walk him to our door.

My son was crumbling right in front of me. *How had I failed him so miserably? Why was this happening to my baby?*

As I knelt there beside the bed that day in the Fall of 2008, I did the only thing I knew to do—pray: *Oh Father, help me! The pain is so deep and real. How do I live above this? I suffer for another's pain. He's my child. How do I free him from the pain? Not only now, but the pain that awaits him as he tries to make it in the world?*

CHAPTER 1

About Me

Trust in the LORD with all your heart, and lean not on your own understanding; In all your ways acknowledge Him, and He shall direct your paths.

PROVERBS 3:5-6 NKJV

In order for you to best understand the story contained in this book, you have to know a little about me. Before Ross was born, my life was centered, of course, around me. My goals in life concerned, of course, me. My ambitions were to go to college and graduate with skills that would lead to a high paying career. I was performance driven.

I can remember back to the first grade, not wanting to take home any papers that were not A's. I would get rid of them, one way or the other, before I made it home. I wanted to please my parents and their acceptance, or rather their praise, was a big deal to me.

Maybe this was a function of being the oldest child in my family. By birth order definition, oldest children have a tendency to be higher achievers than younger siblings. (Don't get offended, those of you who are younger siblings. I'm just repeating what research suggests.) I don't remember my parents prodding me to study or do homework. The mere thought of going to school unprepared was something I did not want to experience. There was just something inside of me that hated failing.

Academically, I excelled. I graduated with the highest grade point average in my class. I was the high school yearbook editor my senior year. My efforts resulted in a full ride scholarship to any school of my choice within the state of New Mexico.

After high school, I left my small rural town and went to college, though not in New Mexico (I should have rethought that one). In college, I excelled again academically. I received the Woman of the Year award. I was a residential assistant. I served as vice president in student government. I was co-chairman of the Race Across America qualifying event. The list of my activities and achievements could go on and on.

I graduated college with a bachelors degree in business administration with an emphasis in marketing. My first job was selling radio ads in Garden City, Kansas. I was successful and set sales records, though I'm not sure how I did that. I was an absolute failure at role play in our sales meetings. I'm sure my co-workers and supervisors thought, *How does she ever sell anything?*

There is one thing I need to point out in all of this: My achievements were a result of application. I was a committed student. I worked hard and spent the time to learn the material. I applied myself. I was not naturally intelligent. I was just disciplined to do the work.

I'm a Type A personality with a day planner and a To Do list. I'm not an impromptu person; I like to have a plan. I like to have a schedule and follow the schedule. I want my ducks to be in a row and if possible, I like to know the kind and color of the ducks.

So now that I have established a little background about myself, you can see that I was nowhere near prepared for what lay in store for me!

CHAPTER TWO

Pregnancy

"For I know the plans I have for you," declares the LORD, "plans to prosper you and not to harm you, plans to give you hope and a future."

JEREMIAH 29:11

I got married in July of 1993 and found out in September of 1995 that I was pregnant. I was elated! It was a planned pregnancy. I wanted a baby so badly. I couldn't wait to know if it was a boy or a girl. What would it look like? Would it be intelligent, an athlete, or maybe both? My mind took me through a thousand "what ifs," but the one thing I knew was, I loved this baby!

I didn't have a normal pregnancy. The pregnancy "glow" was nowhere to be found. The only glow I had came from the sweat beads on my forehead when my stomach once again decided to reject partially digested food. They may call it morning sickness, but the nausea lasted all day. I felt awful, like I had the flu that never went away. Not only did I feel bad, I looked bad. Some say they never looked or felt better than when they were pregnant. What's up with that? My face broke out with multiple large blemishes. My normally blond hair turned dark. My cheeks lost all of their natural color. I snored profusely, and even started drooling. Yuck! I was tired and very emotional.

At nine weeks into my pregnancy, I started bleeding. I was afraid I was going to miscarry. My mom had had several miscarriages and I was hoping this was not something that was hereditary. I lay in bed, still as I possibly could be, as if moving might cause a harmful effect. I just lay there and prayed.

I had a doctor's appointment scheduled for the next day. At the appointment, my doctor checked me and said, "Time will tell." Like that's encouraging. I wanted someone to say, "You're going to be fine," but I kept faith and the bleeding eventually stopped. I think this situation made me realize more than ever how precious life is, and just how quickly it can be taken away.

My morning sickness, or shall I call it "day sickness," continued. Every day was a struggle to get up and go to work. I worked at two museums doing public relations and marketing work. I had a 45-minute commute and often times, I had to pull over alongside the road in the freezing cold and vomit. I couldn't even eat my favorite foods. I guess if I look on the bright side,

I didn't gain very much weight during my pregnancy—only 22 pounds by my delivery date.

Spring rolled around and I welcomed the rain. It is almost always wet in Missouri in the springtime. I've always loved the rain. It is calming to me. Work kept me real busy and this was a good thing. It kept me focused on what needed to be done and made the time go by quickly.

A week before my delivery date, my mom came to stay with me. She lives in Dalhart, Texas. This was her first grandchild and she didn't want to miss a thing. She had me out walking laps around the neighborhood because she wanted to see that baby. It didn't work. The doctors decided to induce labor a few days before my due date. My stomach wasn't growing as it should and I was not gaining as much weight as expected in my last trimester.

William Ross Phillips was born April 29, 1996, at Heartland Hospital in St. Joseph, Missouri. I was at the hospital at six that morning and they started the inducement about seven. Ross was welcomed at 2:01 p.m. He was nineteen and a half inches long and weighed five pounds and fourteen ounces—not very big for a full term baby. I had elected to do a natural delivery. (Big mistake!) My doctor said that medication would delay labor and he felt that natural was the best approach. I did my breathing as I had learned in class, but the pain was intense.

I finally made it through labor only to find out there were other complications. I had what they called a calcified placenta. The placenta was stuck internally and did not pass after the baby was born. I experienced the worst pain I had ever felt as the doctor tried to pull out the placenta. They took me to surgery and performed an emergency procedure to remove the placenta. They were pushing me through doors and everyone was talking to each other like they do in the movies. It was very unsettling. I didn't know what was wrong with me or what they were going to do about it. The last thing I remember was counting backwards as they put me to sleep.

When I came to in the recovery room, my initial impression was that I could feel heat. I guess they had put a heat lamp on me, though I'm not sure why. I think it had something to do with the healing process and stopping the bleeding. I felt like I was in one of those dreams where you are in a compromising position without any underwear on. (Has anyone else ever had those dreams?) They soon took me back to my room. I remember feeling so weak. That morning, I had also begun suffering from a sinus infection. I couldn't breathe very well and had drainage running down my throat. If you've given birth to a child, you know this is not the time you want to be coughing!

Upon being wheeled into my room, I saw that my mom was holding Ross and she said, "I think he's hungry!" I was so excited to see my baby and hold him.

I couldn't believe he was finally here. He looked so perfect. I think all parents are relieved once the counting of the ten toes and ten fingers is successfully completed for their child. Ross had started to fuss, and though all I really wanted to do was sleep, I tried to give breast feeding my best shot. I felt exhausted, but was so thankful that Ross had made it into the world and that he was healthy. As I held him close and he began to eat, I will never forget the feeling I had: The intense love, deep in my soul that was there for that child.

I finished feeding Ross and they took him back to the nursery about 9:00 p.m. I was ready to lay my head on a pillow and rest. I had had enough excitement that day. My mom left for the evening and said she would be back in the morning. I was so glad she had been there with me. Her presence gave me a lot of comfort. I drifted off to sleep at about 10:00 p.m.

At approximately 11:00 p.m., in came the nurse. She was pushing Ross in his roller bed and said she was bringing him back to me because he was screaming and keeping all the other babies awake. I thought to myself, *What? You can't bring him back to me. I'm tired. Have you forgotten the whole surgery thing? I need some sleep.* But without hesitation, I held my baby. He ate and then slept for a little while. Then he ate and slept a little while longer. And so the story began, eat and sleep... a little while.

Motherhood
Blissful...or not!

So many new mothers feel overwhelmed and emotional, especially when it's your first child and you have nothing with which to compare the experience. You have spent your full existence in life up to this point worrying about and taking care of yourself. Now taking a bath or going to the restroom alone is a rare occurrence. You're now taking showers as fast as you can – if you even get to take a shower—and forget about having time to shave your legs. The skin that stretched to accommodate your bundle of joy is now hanging over the top of your pants. The only thing that really excites you these days is the thought of a nap – alone!

I now welcomed cone-shaped breast aerators that made me look like something straight out of a Madonna music video, even though they made me look ridiculous, because the touch of my bra on my raw breasts was more painful than I could handle. I found myself doing things I would have sworn I would never do. I would shamelessly whip a breast out in public and offer it to my son, just for a moment's peace. Anything to stop the crying.

CHAPTER THREE

Infancy and the First Year

Come to me, all you who are weary and burdened, and I will give you rest. Take my yoke upon you and learn from me, for I am gentle and humble in heart, and you will find rest for your souls. For my yoke is easy and my burden light.

MATTHEW 11: 28-30

Ross's Infancy Characteristics

1. Cried a lot and for no apparent reason
2. High maintenance
3. All consuming of my time
4. Difficult to console
5. Did not require much sleep
6. Strong willed and would not cry it out
7. Loved rocking and swinging
8. Loved watching movies, even at a few months old

We left the hospital on Thursday morning. They had kept me an extra day since I had the surgery. I had read that infants usually slept a lot. I was looking forward to the rest myself. However, this was not the case with my baby. Ross's screaming was piercing. He seldom seemed content. I tried everything I knew to do. I checked his diaper, I fed him, made sure he was the right temperature, made sure all the tags had been removed from his clothes so that nothing was poking him. I followed a strict diet of "do not eat foods" when you are nursing. I read everything I could find on colic and things that might help, nothing worked. There were times when Ross was not crying, but those times only came through constant effort and never lasted very long.

Night after night, infomercial after infomercial, I sat in the rocking chair trying to console my baby. He seemed calmer and less irritable when I was rocking him. He clearly liked rhythmic movement.

Leaving the house became more difficult. I watched as other parents of infants took their child to dinner and the child slept in their car seat for the duration of the meal. I remember seeing a parent taking an infant into a movie theatre as multiple thoughts ran through my head. *How is this possible? What are they doing that I am not? How do they seem so together? Why am I failing so miserably?*

When Ross was a few weeks old, a co-chairman of mine from the museum wanted to come over and talk to me about an upcoming event. I tried to discourage her from coming by, telling her that my baby was pretty fussy. She assured me that would be fine and we would just work as long as we could. She came over, but ended up leaving about thirty minutes after she arrived. I think we talked for a total of five minutes and the rest of the time was spent trying to keep Ross from screaming. My colleague sat there just looking at me, or at least that's what it felt like. I kept wondering what I was doing wrong. I felt embarrassed. When I was around other people, Ross's constant crying made me more nervous than normal. I guess I thought his crying was a reflection of my lack of parenting skills. By those standards, I must be the world's worst mother!

Going to bed was no longer part of my routine. If I made it to my bed at all, it was only for periods of time just long enough to catch a minimal amount of sleep. Nights and days rolled into each other with no sense of routine. I felt like I was losing my mind. I was so alone and defeated. I was so tired I didn't have the strength to cry, silent tears that came when I blinked, ran down my face. A pain took up residence in my soul, so deep it made me sick. I experienced complete exhaustion and frustration. Was this what they meant by "the joys of motherhood"?

What happens when the hype of the peaceful baby sleeping in the crib turns into the reality of a screaming baby who never sleeps and is difficult or almost impossible to console? Then what? My reality was not the same as that idealized in commercials. When you are pregnant and you are dreaming of holding your baby, the baby isn't screaming in the dream. You don't think about sitting on the toilet, nursing while you go to the bathroom. No, you read every parenting book and you come to believe that if I follow these guidelines, this will be a piece of cake. If you follow these certain steps, then in just a matter of time the child will go to sleep on their own; fuss for a few minutes, maybe, then drift off into peaceful slumber. But what happens when this doesn't work? There was no chapter in the books that I read that said, "If your child screams relentlessly...this is what you do." Remember, I'm a Type A personality, I had done my homework, I had looked. Any suggestions I did find claiming to aid with a screaming child, failed to work.

I was now living in survival mode. All I could think about was getting from one moment of sleep to the next. I was so tired, I fell asleep in the shower. My eyes burned and often watered. I ran into door facings. I felt like I was in a fog. I couldn't focus. My body ached like I had the flu.

The crying seemed to never end. Although it's difficult to admit, there were days I thought about jumping out a window. Not that I wanted to end my life, I just felt like I was going insane. The constant thought, *What am I doing wrong?* went through my head hour after hour.

Once Ross did go to sleep, he was restless. I remember the echoing words said to me by well-meaning people, "He will sleep when he gets tired." What, exactly, is that supposed to mean?! Everyone, no matter how young or old, has to have sleep, right? That didn't seem to be true of Ross. How can an infant survive with no sleep? For that matter, how can anyone survive with no sleep?

Two Months

My sister was getting married and we went home to go to the wedding. This was an eight-hour drive. I'm not sure how many of those eight hours in the car Ross cried, but my nerves were frayed and my hands trembled by the time we arrived.

The trip was a disaster. Ross cried through the whole rehearsal. He cried through the entire wedding. At the reception at my dad's house, I got a piece of wedding cake (my absolute favorite). Hours later, a dried out, half-eaten piece of wedding cake still laid on the plate. There was no reprieve. Ross just cried and cried!

While I was visiting for the wedding, some of my extended family came to visit the baby. As usual, Ross was fussy, irritable and all consuming. My aunt turned to me with a look of disgust and said, "I don't see how you deal with that." I didn't know what to say. I felt my shoulders sink and all I could think of to say in response was, "What do you want me to do, put him back?" To be honest, I didn't know how I did it either. I was on edge, completely exhausted and didn't know what to do.

Going Back to Work

A whole book could be written about all the emotions a mother feels about leaving her child. I was no exception. Part of me was excited about going back to work. I loved working. I had never envisioned my life without working. That's why I had worked so hard in school, right? But now, I was experiencing all sorts of feelings and emotions I didn't even understand. (It could have been from the lack of sleep!) I was uneasy about leaving Ross. Could his care providers handle him? Would they be loving and kind when he cried and cried?

I was blessed to have found someone to care for Ross who loved babies. She wasn't able to have children of her own and adored spending time with Ross. She loved him. Looking back I know that she was God sent, this is the only explanation. She kept only Ross and all her attention was devoted to his every need. She rocked him, took him on strolls outside, read to him, and spent her hours entertaining him. She watched Ross for about a year. She commented on several occasions that he was the smartest and most alert baby she ever saw.

Moving to Kansas

When Ross was about one year old, we decided to move to Wichita, Kansas. I was not excited about the move to Kansas. When we had moved to Missouri just two years before, there was no family close by and I knew no one. Through my involvement with the museums, I eventually made a lot of friends and was not anxious to leave now and start the process over again. This meant new doctors, a new pediatrician, learning my way around another city, and frankly, I was worn out.

We moved to an apartment while we waited for our house to sell. Living in an apartment with any one year old is challenging, especially when the one year old is fussy, high maintenance and rarely sleeps. Ross was active, often seeming to have an endless supply of energy. He had one volume and it was loud! When he did sleep, he was restless and never seemed to be really well rested. As most mothers know, a tired baby equals a fussy baby and a fussy baby equals exhausted parents.

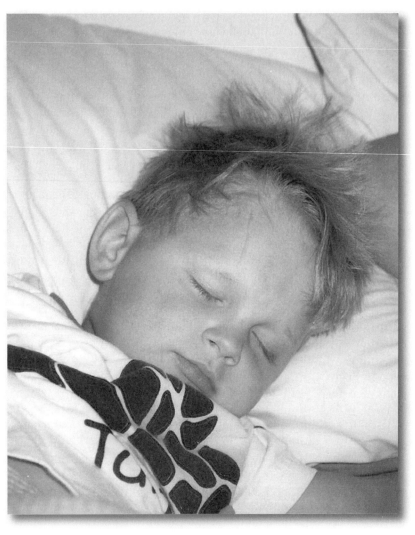

Since birth, Ross has been a restless sleeper.
He's as active when he's asleep as when he's awake.

CHAPTER FOUR

The Toddler Years

Train a child in the way he should go, and when he is old he will not turn from it.

PROVERBS 22:6

Ross's Characteristics During the Toddler Years

1. Difficult

2. Cried a lot and very hard to console

3. Strong-willed and defiant, would not cry it out

4. Loved books, being rocked, and watching movies

5. Did not require a lot of sleep

6. Difficulty going to sleep and then was restless

7. Lined up plastic animals in particular sequence

8. Re-enacted scenes from movies

9. Difficult to take in public places

10. Demanded a lot of attention, wanted to be close to me

11. Always on the go, very active

12. Loud

By the time Ross reached the age of two, he could communicate his strong preferences to me. It was clear he liked repetition. I would read the same books over and over. His favorite was *The Foot Book,* by Dr. Seuss. I read this book hundreds of times. Probably more. Let me give you a sense of what the book is like...

> *Left foot*
> *Left foot*
> *Right foot*
> *Right*
> *Feet in the morning*
> *Feet at night*
> *Wet foot*
> *Dry foot*
> *Low foot*
> *High foot*
> *Front feet*

Back feet
Red feet
Black feet

Left foot
Right foot
Feet Feet Feet
How many, many feet you meet.

In addition to liking to hear the same books over and over, Ross also liked to watch the same movies time and again. He watched them over and over and over. Ultimately, I found that television had the most calming effect on Ross. He would actually not cry, sit still, and watch it. It was like he craved it.

Along the way, everyone had a discipline theory to offer that would "straighten Ross out." You know what I mean, the "if you would just" approach. It was even suggested that a good old-fashioned spanking surely would do the trick. People are so critical. The criticism I received was rough for me to take. I already felt like a failure. The truth is, I couldn't control Ross.

I want to point out that all these characteristics I've mentioned that Ross was displaying can be seen in any child at one time or another. But when these problems are consistent and seem to be excessive, a problem may exist. Such was the case with Ross.

Sixteen Elephants

It was summertime and Ross and I packed up to make an 8-hour road trip. I knew before I left that the trip would be a challenge, but I told myself that I could do it.

Ross didn't like being in the car seat, as most children don't, but with the help of "Silly Songs" and another tape we had listened to a hundred times at least, I thought I could occupy him for part of the time. Ross and I usually traveled alone and this made it especially challenging, since Ross was in the back seat and I couldn't readily hand him what he decided he needed at that moment. Ross wasn't patient and was relentless in his requests. For road trips, I would pack treats, all his favorites and several sippie cups of drinks. The sippie cups would be filled with apple juice or Tang. Ross was very specific about what he liked and disliked and a road trip wasn't the time to start new introductions. By the time we would reach our destination, there would be about five sippie cups in the floor, all half drunk, that Ross had decided to send airborne over the side of his chair when he was tired of holding them, only to want them again once they hit the floor. Ross had favorite sippie cups, of course. I guess the color and the feel of the cup were pleasing for one reason or another, because a drink from his "favorite cup" was always more pleasing to him.

I'm sure many of you are thinking, *If that was my child I would....* Oh, do be careful what you say! Once upon a time, those words were uttered from my lips. I had been very dogmatic about what I would and wouldn't accept in a child's behavior. I had firm boundaries set in my mind that I would not tolerate being violated. But then I had Ross and I decided that if I wanted to survive, I was going to have to use my energy to address the big things and let the smaller things go.

For this trip, I had packed Ross's favorite toys, or shall I say "things." I packed his blue blankie, a grey elephant that made a noise when you squeezed it, and a green squishy alligator. He liked to carry things in his hands.

While we were visiting, my sister gave Ross a tube of animals, safari animals that included elephants, tigers, lions, zebras and hippos. He played with the toy animals the entire time we were on our trip. I noticed he was more content than normal and that playing with the animals held his attention longer than any other toy he had ever played with. I had never before found anything that had kept him occupied or entertained for any period of time. When Ross played with something, he played a matter of minutes, then he was done and on to the next thing. But this was different. On the way home I looked back at him and he had lined up the tigers and the lions on the bar across the front of his car seat, lions together, then a space, and then tigers together. He gazed at the animals intently. What was most observable was that he wasn't as agitated as normal. He was quieter and less fussy. Of course, I couldn't make sudden stops or turns or I would have to pull over and retrieve the animal that had fallen off and put it right back in the exact spot it had fallen from.

By the time Ross was almost three, he had acquired sixteen elephants. They were plastic elephants of various sizes. I noticed he lined them up on the coffee table the same way every time. One day I knocked over a few of the elephants with the vacuum cleaner cord and placed them back on the coffee table in a different order. When I came back in the room, Ross had moved them back in the proper order. At the time I didn't give it much thought. I just knew Ross really liked playing with those animals and he preferred them to be lined up a certain way. Everywhere we went, he was looking to add animals to his collection. But not just any animals, only the animals he showed an interest in. Ross never actually played with the animals. He either held them in his hands, or lined them up.

In addition to lining up animals in a sequential pattern, Ross had another love—movies. He had his favorites and watched them over and over. This had a calming effect on him. The most amazing thing was that when Ross was watching a movie, he was quiet. From a very early age, movies held a certain fascination for him. He memorized the words to the movie and said them back to me by rote memory. This made Ross sound much older than he actually was. He had an ever-increasing vocabulary and seemed to be ahead of the guidelines in the "What to Expect" books by a decent margin.

However, behaviorially, Ross was still behind. He still didn't sleep well and seemed fitful when he slept. He was fussy and never seemed to be appropriately rested. He had dark circles under his eyes and I knew he had to be tired. In my opinion, there are very few people who could operate on the amount of sleep Ross was getting, much less a three year old. When he did sleep, it was only for short periods of time and his sleep was constantly interrupted by periods of crying. He just never seemed to "give it up" and sleep.

Ross has always had a special connection with animals.

CHAPTER FIVE

Preschool Years

Let your speech always be with grace, seasoned with salt,
that you may know how you ought to answer each one.

COLOSSIANS 4:6 NKJV

Ross's Pre-K Characteristics

1. Counts things

2. Dominates conversations

3. Has difficulty waiting his turn

4. Talks a lot

5. Two volumes—loud and louder

6. Doesn't seem to listen well

7. Hyperactive

8. Demands a lot of attention

9. Ritualistic

10. Loves to draw

As Ross aged, he added more rituals to his daily routine. Playing "Pooh Bear Gets Stuck" was a ritual that he developed that he had to observe before eating each meal. He loved watching Winnie the Pooh and he latched on to this particular story segment, which is based on scenes from the movie, *Winnie the Pooh and the Honey Tree* (Disney, 1996). Ross would play the role of Pooh and I would play the role of Rabbit. The scene had to be played out in exact sequence. Forget about skipping a line to speed things up or you'll find yourself back at the beginning starting the role play over.

Pooh Bear (aka Ross):	"Is anybody at home?"
Rabbit (aka Me):	"No! You needn't shout so loud. I heard you quite well the first time."
Pooh Bear:	"Bother! Isn't there anybody here at all?"
Rabbit:	"Nobody."
Pooh Bear:	"Rabbit, isn't that you?"
Rabbit:	"No!"
Pooh Bear:	"Why, hello Rabbit."

Rabbit :	"Are you hungry Pooh Bear? Honey or condensed milk with your bread?"
Pooh Bear:	"Both."

At this point, Ross would eat his food. When he was finished, the game continued.

Rabbit:	"Are you sure you won't have any more?"
Pooh Bear:	"Is there any more?"
Rabbit:	"No."
Pooh Bear:	"Well I must be going."

Ross would walk over to the door and pretend he was stuck. He would yell out "I'm a Pooh Bear wedged in great tightness!" I would then have to go over and pretend I was pulling him out of the hole in which he was stuck. He would tell me to go get Christopher Robin.

The drill would continue with me pushing and pulling Ross to "unstick him from the hole." Finally, Ross would yell "Pop!" as if he were suddenly released, and the ritual was over.

This was a lot of work to do to get Ross to eat a peanut butter and jelly sandwich. Let me rephrase that. This was a lot of work to do to finish what was already a long and arduous process. Even making a sandwich wasn't easy. The sandwich had to be made on a certain type of bread with a certain type of peanut butter and jelly, and had to be cut corner to corner. Heaven forbid you make the mistake of cutting the sandwich down the middle!

Every Kind of Dinosaur Imaginable

Ross developed an obsession with dinosaurs. He wanted dinosaur books, dinosaur figures, and dinosaur movies. He drew dinosaurs and literally talked hours every day about dinosaurs. He had an extensive vocabulary and used words that seemed strange coming from the mouth of a four-year-old.

Ross loved going to the video store and, as with most everything else, picked the same movies over and over. One of his favorites was *National Geographic's Really Wild Animals: Dinosaurs and Other Creature Features* (Grasshoff, 1996). The movie started with the words, "Featuring dinosaurs, maggots, cockroaches, komodo dragons and dung beetles. Those dinos were really, really wild." By rote memory, Ross would quote Paleontologist Robert Bakker:

T-rex, jaw wide open.

These teeth are not sharp, they are like railroad spikes. They are armor piercing teeth for crushing through the hide and bones of a triceratops and these jaws, no animal in the world has evolved stronger jaws. Incredibly wide with muscles so strong that this T-rex could reach down and pick up a bull Indian Rhino and shake it like a rag doll. That's how it would kill... bite, penetrate, and shake the animal to death, then crush up its prey in chunks small enough to swallow.

Over and over, Ross repeated this phrase verbatim from the video. When he met new people, instead of engaging in a conversation, he would just recite this monologue over and over. People would look at me, and of course, I just smiled. I realize this really didn't sound like something a four-year-old would say.

Danny and the Dinosaur

Danny and the Dinosaur was a book that I read over and over to Ross. One night when Ross was about four years old, we sat down in the chair to read *Danny and the Dinosaur* yet again, but this time he wanted to read the book to me. Fifty-six pages of text he recited to me without missing a word! He couldn't read—he had memorized the book. I was amazed.

Rhett Is Born

I gave birth to my second child when Ross turned four. His name is Rhett Joseph Phillips. I will always consider Rhett a gift from God. Had God not intervened and said I was having another child, I would not be blessed to have Rhett. I remember when I found out I was pregnant, I fell to my knees and wept. I said, "God, You say in Your Word You will never give us more than we can handle. In case You haven't noticed, I'm not doing that great of a job here. I'm an emotional wreck. I haven't had uninterrupted sleep in so long, I don't even know what it would be like. I have no help, no family that lives close, and I don't know how I am going to do this." I just began to pray every day that God would give me strength and a good-tempered baby who liked to sleep!

One of my biggest worries about having another baby concerned the time I would go to the hospital to give birth, which would mean leaving Ross alone at night with someone else. I know that sounds like a strange thing to worry about, but dealing with Ross at night was that intense an experience.

When Rhett was born, I noticed right away that he had a different temperament than Ross. He was much more relaxed and easier to console. He seemed happy. He actually slept! At this point, I was still getting up at night with Ross, more so than with the newborn baby.

Ross welcomed Rhett home and seemed to watch him intently. Ross was good to his little brother and loved feeding him his bottle. As Rhett got older, Rhett would wrestle in the floor with Ross, and Ross loved it.

Please, Not Wal-Mart

Trips to Wal-Mart were always entertaining. I can say they were entertaining now as I think back on them, but at the time these trips took place, they were stressful and embarrassing. Ross often spoke the first thing that popped into his head, so you can imagine the number of times I tried to intervene or steer him down a different aisle. If I saw anyone on an aisle with anything about them that seemed out of the ordinary, I tried to avoid them to curb Ross's questions. However, there were often too many people in the store to try to avoid. Ross would ask questions to satisfy his curious mind but those questions would leave me apologizing in their wake and feeling helpless.

One day as we were waiting for our food at the McDonald's counter inside Wal-Mart, along came a lady who was grossly overweight. I cut a look at Ross that said, *Don't...please don't.* As the lady approached the counter, Ross said, "Mom I'm not going to say a word about how big that lady is, but she looks like she weighs a ton." Yes, once again I was left apologizing, knowing my son had dashed someone's feelings on the rocks.

On yet another of our Wal-Mart adventures, we were walking down an aisle and a lady was coming toward us. She was extremely overweight to the point that her stomach was hanging down to her thighs. Ross turned to the lady and asked, "What is that hanging down there on your legs?" I smiled and apologized profusely for my son's question. I talked to Ross repeatedly about not saying things that would hurt other people's feelings, even if his questions or observations were true and obvious. Please know that Ross never said things to intentionally hurt others. But we learned early on not to ever ask Ross a question if we didn't want an honest answer. He will not lie and will often tell you truths you would just as soon not hear.

Ross had an issue with wiping his own bottom. He absolutely refused to do it. This may seem like a big problem, but I had had such a problem getting him to go poopy in the potty in the first place that this didn't seem like that big of an issue. When Ross was being potty trained, he was able to master peeing in the potty, but the rest didn't go as well. He would hold his poopy for days. When he did try to go in the potty, the whole process literally freaked him out. He would cry and say, "No..no..no!" I had to eventually use suppositories to get him to go. So you can see, after clearing that hurdle, and trust me it took a long time, the wiping thing I could handle.

Anyway, back to Wal-Mart. One day I was standing in the check-out line with Rhett in his infant carrier and Ross standing beside me. About halfway through checkout, Ross announced, "I gotta poop!"

I said, "Wait just a minute."

"I can't wait, I gotta poop!" With Ross, waiting was never a virtue. I was standing right in front of the restrooms in my check-out line, so I told him to go inside the bathroom and wait for me. Of all the times for my son to finish his business in a hurry, this was not one I would have chosen. Before I knew it, Ross came out of the bathroom with his pants around his ankles, saying "Come wipe me! Come wipe me!" The clerk just looked at me and I shook my head. All I wanted to do was get out of that store. I didn't pay attention nor would I have cared if she charged me fifty dollars more than my bill was supposed to be. I just wanted out of there.

One of Ross's favorite things has always been spending time with his Auntie and cousins. Pictured L to R: Ross Phillips, Connor Holiski, Holly Holiski (Ross's Auntie), Halle Holiski, and Rhett Phillips.

First Diagnosis: OCD

The LORD is close to the brokenhearted and saves those who are crushed in spirit.

PSALM 34:18

When Ross was four and a half years old, I was outside washing the window on the door to the kitchen when he had a meltdown and became hysterical. I thought he was going to break through the glass to get to me. He could clearly see me. It was just that the door was closed and he was separated from me. What he was experiencing was complete panic. He wasn't crying because he wasn't getting his way or because he needed something – it was because he couldn't get to me. I had known for some time that Ross was unique and that what I experienced with him wasn't typical, but what I didn't want to admit was that maybe underneath the "uniqueness" lay a real problem.

I knew I needed a professional to evaluate Ross to let me know how I could help my child, but to be honest, I didn't even know what kind of doctor to see. We had recently moved to Tulsa. I didn't know many people and didn't even really know the kinds of questions to ask to get me where I needed to go. I went through my days in a haze and all I really wanted was sleep and a little peace and quiet. By this time, I was so numb that I really didn't even cry that much anymore.

Ross's father and I took Ross to see a child psychologist in Tulsa. He spent some time with Ross and remarked that he is a very brilliant boy. Ross drew some pictures for him that were of Pooh Bear and Piglet. As the doctor asked him questions, Ross ran about as if he were on speed. He climbed on the furniture. He jumped from one chair to another and paid little attention to the doctor. The doctor tilted his head to the side and said, "Maybe you should consider the Tulsa University School for the Gifted."

While the doctor implied that there were indicators of ADHD, he didn't concretely diagnose anything. I thought to myself, *That's it? That's all you can tell me? I finally brought myself to seek help, and that's all you can say?*

We enrolled Ross in K-4 Preschool at Rejoice Christian School. Just the fact that the school had the word "Christian" in its name made me feel better. Ross was already five, but I didn't think he was behaviorally ready for kindergarten. I wanted him to go to preschool more for the social aspects of school than the academic aspects. Academically Ross seemed to be fine, if not advanced, but socially, we were behind the curve. I wanted Ross to learn to interact with other children, to learn to wait his turn, and to learn when it is appropriate to talk and when it isn't.

Ross's preschool teacher was Ms. Shade. I communicated openly with her my concerns about Ross. I'm sure she could sense my nervousness about him starting school. He was a handful, and I knew it, but Ms. Shade seemed to handle him well. One day when I was inquiring about his progress, she said, "Dee, when we enter a room, he counts the ceiling tiles and the outlets in the room. Have you noticed this behavior at home?" I can't honestly say that I had observed that specific behavior, but the rigidity of his behavior had been prevalent since birth. This particular observation just added one more piece to the puzzle.

The school was hosting a free seminar about ADHD (attention deficit hyperactivity disorder). Since the child psychologist we consulted mentioned this as a possible diagnosis for Ross's condition, I decided to check it out. The speaker was Dr. Rick Walton. He lectured on the symptoms and problems associated with ADHD. Although some of the symptoms matched Ross's behavior, others didn't. I decided to book an appointment with Dr. Walton at his clinic and have him evaluate Ross.

March 2002

When Dr. Walton met with Ross, he performed a series of tests. He asked Ross questions directly and then directed questions toward me and Ross's father. He also had a questionnaire for Ross's teacher to complete.

Once Dr. Walton had completed his evaluation, we met with him and he asked us if we were familiar with OCD, or more formally, obsessive-compulsive disorder. For me, this diagnosis came out of the blue. I had already prepared myself for the ADHD diagnosis, but OCD? At the time, I didn't even know what OCD was. The only thing I really knew about OCD was that it often manifested itself in a propensity to be obsessed with washing your hands. That's pretty limited knowledge, I know. But once Dr. Walton presented us with this diagnosis, I went to work to find out as much about the condition as I could.

The American Psychiatric Association's *Diagnostic and Statistical Manual of Mental Disorders* (DSM), is used by mental health professionals to assist in the diagnosis of disorders. These diagnostic standards are established to ensure that people are appropriately diagnosed. I read through the DSM criteria for OCD and found that obsessions are defined by the following:

- Recurrent and persistent thoughts, impulses, or images that are experienced at some time during the disturbance, as intrusive and inappropriate and that cause marked anxiety and distress.

§ The thoughts, impulses, or images are not simply excessive worries about real-life problems.

§ The person with these obsessions attempts to ignore or suppress such thoughts, impulses, or images, or to neutralize them with some other thought or action.

§ The person recognizes that the obsessional thoughts, impulses, or images are a product of his or her own mind (not imposed from without as in thought insertion).

With an understanding of the obsession portion of OCD, I now turned my attention to the compulsive issue. The DSM defined compulsions as:

§ Repetitive behaviors (e.g., hand washing, ordering, checking) or mental acts (e.g., praying, counting, repeating words silently) that the person feels driven to perform in response to an obsession, or according to rules that must be applied rigidly.

§ The behaviors or mental acts are aimed at preventing or reducing distress or preventing some dreaded event or situation; however, these behaviors or mental acts either are connected in a realistic way with what they are designed to neutralize or prevent or are clearly excessive.

The DSM went on to say that in OCD, the obsessions or compulsions cause the person with the disorder "marked distress, are time consuming (take more than 1 hour a day), or significantly interfere with the person's normal routine, occupational (or academic) functioning, or usual social activities or relationships." (American Psychiatric Association, *DSM-IV-TR,* 462-463.)

The further I went in my research, the more I saw that many of Ross's characteristics of behavior fit into the information I read, but there was an array of other issues that didn't seem to fit in the OCD mold. I didn't question the diagnosis, I just felt there was more to the problem. For instance, the major impairment in social interactions that Ross manifests didn't seem to be a prominent factor seen in an OCD diagnosis. But after much consideration, we elected to start Ross on medication to assist with OCD.

CHAPTER SEVEN

Second Diagnosis: ADHD

Therefore we also, since we are surrounded by so great a cloud of witnesses, let us lay aside every weight, and the sin which so easily ensnares us, and let us run with endurance the race that is set before us.

HEBREWS 12:1 NKJV

Throughout grade school, we continued to see Dr. Walton. Although we were making some progress, it was clear we still had other issues to address. After further testing, Dr. Walton diagnosed Ross with ADHD in addition to the OCD diagnosis.

I returned to the *American Psychiatric Association Diagnostic and Statistical Manual* (DSM) to review the criteria for ADHD. According to the DSM, for someone to be diagnosed with ADHD, they must exhibit six or more of the symptoms of inattention and six or more symptoms of hyperactivity or impulsivity for at least six months, to a point that is inappropriate for the patient's development level.

The following is the list of possible symptoms of inattention, per the DSM:

- Often does not give close attention to details or makes careless mistakes in schoolwork, work, or other activities.

- Often has trouble keeping attention on tasks or play activities.

- Often does not seem to listen when spoken to directly.

- Often does not follow through on instructions and fails to finish schoolwork, chores, or duties in the workplace (not due to oppositional behavior or failure to understand instructions).

- Often has trouble organizing activities.

- Often avoids, dislikes, or doesn't want to do things that take a lot of mental effort for a long period of time (such as schoolwork or homework).

- Often loses things needed for tasks and activities (e.g., toys, school assignments, pencils, books, or tools).

- Is often easily distracted.

- Is often forgetful in daily activities.

The following is the list of possible symptoms for hyperactivity or impulsivity per the DSM:

- ৯ Often fidgets with hands or feet or squirms in seat when sitting still is expected.

- ৯ Often gets up from seat when remaining in seat is expected.

- ৯ Often excessively runs about or climbs when and where it is not appropriate (adolescents or adults feel very restless).

- ৯ Often has trouble playing or doing leisure activities quietly.

- ৯ Is often "on the go" or often acts as if "driven by a motor".

- ৯ Often talks excessively.

- ৯ Often blurts out answers before questions have been finished.

- ৯ Often has trouble waiting one's turn.

- ৯ Often interrupts or intrudes on others (e.g., butts into conversations or games).

(American Psychiatric Association, *DSM-IV-TR,* 92-93.)

As I reviewed the information I found during my research of ADHD, I saw that Ross definitely exhibited behaviors that were consistent with this diagnosis. He was hyper-verbal, impulsive, couldn't wait his turn and blurted out information. At this point, we added another medication to address the ADHD to the OCD meds Ross was already taking.

Individual Education Program

Ross qualified for an IEP (Individual Education Program) at school. This acronym was something new to me. Up to this point, I didn't even know IEP's existed. I grew up in a small town and my exposure to kids who had disabilities was limited. I remember one particular boy from my kindergarten class who was put in a refrigerator box for interrupting other students and jumping from desk to desk during class. And then there was another unruly boy who was out of control and continually made fun of our elementary principal who had a prosthetic arm. That's about the sum total of my experience with kids who might have needed IEPs!

In my small town, any student who had a recognized learning disability was put in special ed classes. When I was now introduced to the IEP, I was clueless. I didn't have any idea what the function or purpose of such a thing might be. All I knew was that Ross was struggling in school, and I was willing to try anything to get him the help he needed.

In the United States, an Individual Education Program is mandated by the Individuals with Disabilities Education Act (IDEA). Once a child is determined to be eligible for services, an education plan is developed based on the specific needs of that particular child. I came to realize that an IEP could be of great value to Ross. For more information on Individual Education Programs, I would refer you to http://idea.ed.gov.

No White Lies

Ross can't lie. Don't ask Ross a question if you don't want the honest answer because he does not know how to tell a "white" lie!

One day we were walking at the mall, school shopping. Of course this is NOT one of Ross's favorite things, but he is so picky about the clothes he wears that I thought it would be best if he helped pick them out. As we were walking along, he looked at me and said, "Mom, you know I will still love you even though you are losing it."

I said, "What do you mean, 'I'm losing it'?"

Ross said, "Well, you know you are starting to get those lines around your eyes and, well, you know, you don't look as good as you did in your 20's." He proceeded to tell the clerks at the Dillard's check-out counter how much better I used to look and then compared me to a poster hanging in the store, saying that's how my skin used to look! Of course the clerks were laughing at this point, but the funniest part was that Ross had no clue as to why the clerks thought what he said was so funny. He continued on in his monologue format that is common to his manner of speaking. Ross couldn't care less if anyone converses, as long as he gets to tell his story.

So Volatile

On the way home from a doctor's appointment, Ross said he was really, really mad. I asked him what was wrong. He stated there were three things that were really making him mad. Of course, I asked what was bothering him and this was his response:

1. It wasn't going to rain. Earlier that day, the clouds had built and it looked like it was going to rain. It ended up not raining. Ross was mad and added, "You know how I love thunderstorms."

2. It was now 6:30 and the library was closed. Ross was interested in checking out a dinosaur book but now, it was too late to go to the library.

3. He had a lame pencil. It wasn't sharp enough to get his drawing just the way he wanted.

December 2006

Ross wrote a letter to Santa on December 11, 2006. He started the letter by saying he had been good and he asked Santa how he was doing and then he asked for the following things:

Have everyone in Hurricane Katrina
to have a good day.

Santa, you have a good Christmas.

Have everyone to get what they want.

Heal my dad's back on Christmas.

I also want everyone
to be happy on Christmas.

I want to have a good day on Christmas.

Santa, I want most of all
to have a snowy Christmas.

I want you to know that on the week of Christmas when we were visiting my father's house, they had a record snowfall with drifts as high as the roofs of the houses!

What stood out to me the most from Ross's list was that there was not one mention of a toy. It didn't contain a laundry list of material things he wanted, but he prayed instead to have peace and happiness, not only for himself, but for those around him. He has such an amazing heart.

Dear Santa,

I've been a very good boy this year. How are you doing? Send a note with that question and everything you want to say to me. Here below is everything I want you to give me for Christmas.

p.s. Have a good Christmas!

p.s. s. s. Have everyone in Huricane Katrens to have a good day.

p.s. s. Have everyone get what they want.

Dear Santa,
I want dads back to be heels on Christmas. I also want everyone to be happy on Christmas. I want to have a good day on Chrismas. Santa..I want most of all to have a snowy Christmas

By William Ross Phillips

2006

December 2006

CHAPTER EIGHT

My Son Has What?
Diagnosed with Asperger's Syndrome

But those who wait on the LORD shall renew their strength;
they shall mount up with wings like eagles, they shall run
and not be weary, they shall walk and not faint.

ISAIAH 40:31 NKJV

Ross's Characteristics at age 10

1. Moody and hard to please; argumentative; fractious

2. Did not enjoy many activities but loved to draw, loved movies, animals, planets, The Weather Channel and The Discovery Channel

3. Emotional; would have highs and lows in the same few minutes

4. Carried on one-sided conversations; garrulous

5. Did not recognize social cues

6. Easily overwhelmed; trouble organizing things

7. Suffered insomnia

8. Obsessive about certain things, liked order and sequence

9. Limited food choices

10. Prefered to be at home in his "happy place"

11. Very literal

12. Easily distracted and often had his head in the clouds

13. Put words and phrases together in peculiar ways. For instance, would say "maybe 10 or 8 or maybe 6 or 5," would always put the larger number first.

14. Still demanded a lot of attention and instruction, even on everyday tasks

By the time Ross turned 10, he shared some of the same interests any 10-year-old boy might have including Dragon Ball Z, sharks, and dinosaurs. He was also very interested in the weather, especially severe weather like tornados, and he was interested in the universe and planets.

We continued to see Dr. Walton for a period of several years. Although he helped Ross, it seemed we were still missing a piece of the puzzle. Dr. Walton recommended that we seek the assistance of a developmental pediatrician. He referred us to a doctor who was regarded as one of the best in Tulsa.

During this time, I also met with the school counselor. She recommended we have more testing done in order to properly assess the problems we were facing. Ross was now in the third grade. He would frequently "melt down" in class. His third grade teacher described Ross as being extremely talkative, easily agitated and frustrated, cries easily, blurts out answers, has a hard time transitioning from one task to another, and as focusing entirely too much on menial details.

Ross had also started to develop tics. He would clear his throat over and over again, which was no doubt quite distracting to the other students sitting in class. He also would move his fingers as if he were clasping something in mid-air while he was talking. When I asked him about his finger clasping, he didn't even realize he was doing it. Furthermore, the more nervous he became, the more his tics intensified.

Ross's third grade year was a rough one for me, personally. Ross's father and I got divorced. Now, in addition to dealing with the trials of my child who was struggling, I was struggling with issues of my own. I had so much pain in my life, there were days I found it physically difficult to breathe. I mustered up all the energy I had just to get through each day. My life was a mess.

After several months of waiting, the results of the tests the school had performed were in. The test results were sent to the new developmental pediatrician we were seeing. When we met with him, he diagnosed Ross with Asperger's Syndrome, an Autism Spectrum Disorder. I had never even heard of Asperger's Syndrome! OCD and ADHD I had heard of, but Asperger's? Our doctor went over the findings with us and reviewed the characteristic behaviors of a child with Asperger's. The described behaviors matched Ross very well. I hoped this diagnosis was the missing piece of the puzzle we were looking for.

These were a few of the characteristics the doctor listed of a child with Asperger's Syndrome:

- Often says the first thing that pops in their head

- Difficult time interacting with others

- Finds it hard to deal with changes in their environment

- Lengthy, one-sided conversations

- Asks the same thing over and over, and feels anxious if he has to stop

- Doesn't get social cues
- Rigidity in thought
- Has sensory issues
- Poor gross motor skills
- Has difficulty problem solving, analyzing, or synthesizing information
- Pedantic speech
- Has obsessive thoughts and rituals
- Egocentric
- Literal minded
- Easily upset with new routines or quick changes
- Often will interrupt
- Often perceived as rude and too straightforward
- Has a narrow range of interests
- Poor impulse control
- Difficulty with organizational skills
- Unable to read between the lines

Autism Spectrum Disorders

Once I began to research Ross's condition, I found that you don't have to look far to find headlines that show statistics relating to a surge in autism related disorders. Whether we are seeing an actual dramatic increase in autism related disorders or if the increase in diagnoses is just a function of the change in the criteria and definitions used to diagnose the condition, it is clear that there is an increased awareness of the disorder. It is now speculated that about 36 out of every 10,000 people are diagnosed with Asperger's Syndrome, also called Asperger's Disorder. Asperger's Disorder affects four times as many males as females.

Asperger's is a neurological problem. It did not appear in the American Psychiatric Association's manual until 1994. The more I researched, looking for information, the more obvious it became that there are no clear cut answers to questions surrounding this disorder. Doctors and researchers still have little concrete information. They do not know what causes autism and although there are treatment suggestions, there is no cure. Imagine receiving this diagnosis—you have this problem, we don't know why you have this problem, it affects all people differently and to varying degrees, and there is no known cure.

My research led me again to the *American Psychiatric Association Diagnostic and Statistical Manual of Mental Disorders*. From Table 3.5, I found this information on Asperger's Syndrome, which had been adapted for young children. Asperger's Syndrome would be diagnosed if the child manifested at least two of the following behaviors:

- ⑨ Poor eye contact; child doesn't naturally and consistently respond when you smile or frown at him; hard-to-read facial expressions; doesn't pick up on social cues.

- ⑨ Hasn't made friends on his own from preschool or daycare; has difficulty engaging in give-and-take with peers his age; difficulty expanding play beyond his own interests.

- ⑨ Doesn't spontaneously seek out peers to share enjoyment in his creations and projects to demonstrate interests.

- ⑨ Just as happy playing by himself or next to a peer; seems indifferent to another child's interests and/or feelings.

Children with Asperger's would also manifest at least one of the following characteristics:

- ⑨ Child is overly focused on a daily basis on one or two special interests or activities (e.g. dinosaurs/ space/ computer games/ replaying a video by rote).

- ⑨ Repetitive rituals around things like eating, travel, bedtime, and bath.

- ⑨ Finger flicking, spinning, hand flapping.

- ⑨ Can get absorbed in an aspect of his special interest or object but not able to integrate it into the larger context (e.g. may have an interest in brand names of cars but no interest in making up a story about the people who drive these cars).

(American Psychiatric Association, *DSM-IV-TR,* 84.)

Obviously, activities of this nature would make it hard for a child suffering from Asperger's to make friends or fit in with the other children around him. The information I found made it clear that children with Asperger's are not intellectually behind their peers—on the contrary, they often have IQs that are above average. I did find specific mention that children with Asperger's have difficulty with potty training. Validation at last for all I endured in training Ross to poopy in the potty!

Mozart and the Whale

I found the movie, *Mozart and the Whale* (Dimbort, 2005), at the movie store completely by accident. The movie title caught my eye because I had researched Mozart music as a way for Ross to focus and relax. The word "whale" in the title caught my attention because the whale is one of Ross's favorite animals. How surprised I was when I picked up the cover and read that the movie was about two adults with Asperger's Syndrome.

I loved watching the movie. I drew parallels between Ross's behavior and the behaviors the characters displayed in the movie. I thought to myself on several occasions, *That is so Ross.* Lines such as "I want to have contact with people, I'm just pathetically clueless," and "I can't sensor what I say, I just say what I think," hit home in a very real way as I thought about my son. I would recommend this movie to any parent who has a child with an Autistic Spectrum Disorder. It reminds you that you are not alone.

Age 9. Disorders are difficult to understand, because physically the child looks normal. Photo courtesy of Janet Hall.

Ross Phillips

I'm smart, funny, exst-
-rordinary, and good drawer.
I have a mom named See
Phillips and a dad named Phil
Phillips. I lover of God, my
family, and anammals.

I feel sad, happy, and
jellesy. I need all dragon
ball v, and dragon ball books,
and all dragon ball v moives,
and a hundred feet long, and
fifty feet wide flat screen
tv. I fear Meables, hornets,
and bites. I'd like to be
at Yellowstown, and at
Barns and Nobles, and watch
mant Saint Helens. I live in
Oklihoma.

CHAPTER NINE

Fifth Grade

Set your mind on things above, not on earthly things.

COLOSSIANS 3:2

On April 24, 2006, 9 years and 360 days since Ross was born, I decided to put pen to paper and share my experiences in raising a child with an Autistic Spectrum Disorder. It was and still is my hope that I can help someone who desperately needs validation or just give someone another person to relate to who has shared in something similar to what they're going through. There is comfort in knowing that someone else has experienced the same thing you are experiencing.

You might ask what was significant about April 24, 2006 that led me to my decision to record my experiences. This was the day the school called and told me that Ross was stuck in the bathroom and they couldn't get him out. On that day, the school was administering standardized tests and they had locked the classrooms. They explained that they couldn't let Ross back in the classroom so I needed to come and get him. "What, he's in the bathroom?" I said. I didn't fully understand why they couldn't let him back in the classroom but with Ross, I had come to expect the unexpected. So I cancelled my meetings and headed for the school.

Though I didn't divulge to my colleagues why I had to cancel the meeting, all I could think about on the way to the school was *I can't believe I am cancelling a meeting because my son won't come out of the bathroom. How embarrassing.* That day was the proverbial straw that broke the camel's back. I don't know if I really thought I would end up writing a book, but I did know that all of my pent up frustration had to get out, so I sat down at my computer and allowed my feelings to flood the keyboard. It was such a release. Writing down my thoughts and feelings was, in a sense, therapy. It just made me feel better.

As Ross progressed from year to year, school became more difficult for him to manage. We knew that fifth grade was no doubt going to be a challenge. This year he started rotating classes. Instead of having one teacher, one desk, one room, he was now changing classes three times a day. For someone as disorganized as Ross, the more elements of change you enter into his day, the greater the risk of error and problems.

At fifth grade open house, I read an essay Ross had written in class describing himself. One of the things on his list of descriptions was "Lover of God." Wow, Lover of God! My son was so open about his faith. At the tender age of 11, my son had found the one thing that is most precious in the world—love for God. It gave me comfort to know that despite all the challenges I faced with Ross, I had done something right. I had instilled in him the importance of a relationship with God.

Ross had an IEP in place, but when I met with his teachers to discuss problems we were having, I found that little or no modifications were being implemented. The teachers knew very little about his disorders. Knowledge is power. The fact that they knew so little about his disorders left them powerless and made it difficult for them to implement successful strategies.

As fifth grade progressed, so did the problems. I received regular emails from Ross's homeroom teacher. Here's just a sampling of the information she sent to me:

Email One

He's just a different guy from the first part of the year! He's constantly chewing his fingers and will say he knows to stop before it bleeds. He will blurt out a question and not even try to listen to the answer (shut-down mode). His pat response is, "I don't understand," to any type of explanation. It's like there's a thick wall between him and pretty much everything else. He is much more rigid (and I mean much) than he used to be. He slams to a halt if any little thing goes the least bit differently. I can't really put my finger on anything else, but I am very sad to lose the Ross we had earlier. His OCD is REALLY bad right now. If I see anything else I'll let you know. In the meantime, I'll say a prayer. Several.

Email Two

I'm a little knocked off center at Ross's behavior. It's not bad, it's just very different. He is far less "flexible" than he has been in the past and he's having a harder time moving on to the next step in most assignments. He is far more likely to come to a screeching halt if some little thing gets in his way. Up to now he's been better about moving or bypassing something in favor of getting work done. I'm curious about why this is happening. It is creating friction between us, I think. Up to now, I have been able to get him over humps rather easily. Now it's like pulling teeth.

Email Three

I have noticed Ross doing some peculiar things lately. He actually smacked his head and face on his way to the computer to take a test. I have never seen him do that before. He's almost constantly chewing on his fingernails and cuticles (he's done that occasionally in the past, but it's constant now). He really gave the Spanish teacher a hard time, too. Every time she said something in Spanish, he would frantically and repeatedly say, "What did you say? I don't understand! What did she say?" She handled him nicely, but I could tell it surprised her. I don't know if this is anything significant. I just think it's his anxieties trying to find an outlet.

Email Four

Ross can be happy-go-lucky one minute and the next minute, he's in meltdown mode and there's NOTHING I can do to get him out of it. He puts up that wall and there's no getting past it. It's very frustrating for me and for him. Also, he's been using his "condition" as an excuse for lots of things. He'll say, "But I don't want to do it! I won't do it because I've got (he'll use Asperger's or OCD here) and I shouldn't have to do it!" He does it quite a bit lately. Today, he's in a very good mood and I'm walking on eggshells hoping it'll stay that way. That WALL is a demon for me. I try all sorts of things to help him but he just flat can't hear me at that stage. Explaining is a waste of time because he can't hear it. It just makes things worse. But, if I don't at least attempt to explain, he will meltdown even more and will repeatedly say, "I don't get it..." and explode into tears. That's all I know right now.

Tics

Tics were also a problem. In addition to the tic of constantly clearing his throat, Ross developed a tic of clicking his teeth. He didn't even realize he was doing it. This tic was distracting in class. One of his teachers had little tolerance for this behavior and Ross would frequently get in trouble and have to miss recess as punishment for clicking his teeth. This created even more anxiety for him. Ross told me he wanted to give up. He didn't want to live anymore if this was how he had to live. These were words that would pierce any parent. It's so difficult to see a child struggle so hard.

Towards the end of the year, Ross was actually found in the classroom floor curled up in the fetal position, crying. His teacher had to call the counselor to come get him up. His anxiety had reached a point where he just couldn't handle it.

Amazingly, though Ross struggled, he never lost his sense of humor. As a class project, each student had to memorize and recite the Declaration of Independence in front of the class. Ross elected to do his presentation in a "goat boy" voice. The class stood up and cheered at the end of the presentation.

Accelerated Reading Goals

Accelerated Reading Goals, ugh!!! This became a "dirty" word at our house. I always knew a meltdown was on the way when this was brought up. From what was explained to me about the Accelerated Reading program, according to the State of Oklahoma, there was a certain amount of reading and testing that had to be performed by each student. It wasn't the reading that was a problem, it was the kind of reading that was required that was the problem. Ross was a fact finder, a hardcore non-fiction reader. He saw no purpose in reading fiction. If a book wasn't packed with what he considered useful information, he wasn't interested in reading it. The problem was that much of the AR reading was fiction. This created a state of tension for us every night. Ross hated homework and AR reading. It wasn't just that he didn't want to do the homework, but that the homework created a great sense of anxiety for him, which meant a great sense of anxiety was also created for me. There are only so many battles you can fight in a day, and frankly I was worn out!

Bullies

Bullies! No matter where Ross went, bullies seemed to appear out of nowhere. Ross didn't really have any close friends, and maybe that is something bullies look for in a target. In Ross's terms, bullies "look for the one isolated from the herd." Ross's lack of appropriate social skills played into the hands of many bullies. He would do or say something that would leave him wide open for ridicule. The most heartbreaking aspect was that Ross didn't recognize what that "something" was.

Don't Mess with My Legos

At our last visit with Ross's developmental pediatrician, we talked about Ross's numerous obsessions: weather, Dragon Ball Z, coin collecting, the invisible "fuzz" that he believes he must pick from his body, the splinters that no one else can see. "Ritualistic, querulous, habitual, rude, direct and to the point, no tact, state the obvious, demanding, self absorbed, isolated, prefers to play alone, in his own world," these are some of the words that had been used to describe Ross.

Ross, like most of us, is a creature of habit. However his routine was so habitual that if altered, it created a lot of stress for him. The end result was that Ross's stress caused a lot of stress for me, as well.

One of Ross's favorite activities in his late elementary years was playing with Legos. No matter where we went, the Legos went as well. He spent hours creating objects from Legos. Most items were things he created from his own mind, and not with the assistance of instructions. He had the amazing talent of being able to visualize an object and then create it in the real world using Legos.

Did Someone Say "Donuts"?

I swear, Ross could live on donuts and peanut butter and jelly. He was obsessed with donuts. I would actually plan my driving route to be sure I would not drive by a donut store because once Ross saw the donut store, the thought of donuts was imbedded in his mind. He would spend hours begging for donuts.

Barnes and Noble

Ross would rather go to Barnes and Noble than do most any other activity. For his 11th birthday, I asked him if he wanted to have a party or what he wanted to do. He said, "I just want to go to Barnes and Noble." But not just any Barnes and Noble would do, he wanted to go to the one we always went to. Remember, Ross likes predictability and routine. Once, Ross and his brother were invited to a birthday party at Incredible Pizza, a local pizza parlor that has an amazing collection of games and other activities for the patrons to enjoy. He said he didn't want to go to the party, but instead just wanted someone to take him to Barnes and Noble.

Ross watches the same movies over and over and has done that for as long as he's been alive. The problem is, he wants me to watch them with him. He will say, "Watch this Mom. Isn't this cool? Look at this part. Watch his face. Isn't that funny? Why aren't you laughing?" Ross doesn't understand that after 10 times of watching the same segments, it's no longer that funny or amusing. (Though honestly, I didn't find it funny or appealing the first time I watched it anyway.)

One day we were in the car and Ross was giving me a play-by-play of the fight between Goku and Freeza (characters from the cartoon series Dragon Ball Z). This went on for about 15 minutes. No one else in the car was saying a word, we were all just trying to watch Ross's reenactment intensely. He had motions, facial expressions and the whole animated scene going. After I had maintained my attention for as long as I could, I interrupted and said "Honey, we're almost there. Hurry and finish your story."

Ross responded, "Ah Mom, can't we finish? I'm almost halfway through." He had no clue that everyone else had lost interest in his story after the first two minutes.

No Such Thing As a Small Detail

One day while Ross was in the fifth grade, I took the boys to meet the bus. We waited and waited but the bus never came. I decided to take the boys to school, so they wouldn't be tardy. When we reached the front of the subdivision we saw a plethora of emergency vehicles. Police car lights were flashing. There was an ambulance and at least three fire trucks. I pulled over and asked a lady standing by the road what had happened and she said a child had had their foot ran over.

In my mind, the presence of all those emergency vehicles was a little excessive for an injured foot. But as we left the subdivision, Ross said, "This is the worst day ever." I told him we should focus on the positive and be glad that the child was going to be allright. He replied, "You don't know. A child could potentially lose a limb over this deal!" His mind seemed to migrate to the negative. Downplaying the event didn't seem to have much of an impact on him.

Social Skills Group (Summer 2008)

Between fifth and sixth grade, I decided to sign Ross up for a social skills class. Although I wasn't sure where the class would lead, I decided to give it a try. I was excited for the opportunity to meet other parents who were experiencing the same challenges that I faced and was interested in Ross being able to identify with other children as he would say, "of his own kind."

Before the first class, as we were waiting, in walked a boy and his mother. The boy walked in with his head down, playing a hand held video game. He wasn't interested in observing his surroundings and sat in a chair intently focused on his game.

I sat there studying each move the other Asperger's children made, trying to draw parallels in behavior similar to Ross's. The need to constantly have something to occupy their time was evident. Not one child walked in and sat down without something in their hands.

On the third visit to social skills class, Ross forgot to wear shoes. I observed a conversation between three of the boys, which took place while all three boys were engaged in other activities. Ross was playing his hand held Yahtzee game. Another boy was playing his video game, and the third boy was drawing on a magnetic Magnadoodle. The conversation topic concerned the hand held Yahtzee game. Ross declared he was the "King of Yahtzee," to which the other boy replied, "No, I am the king of Yahtzee. Yahtzee is a game of chance and strategy, and at times, pure luck."

The boy playing the video game, while never looking up from his game, responded, "I've never played Yahtzee, but I am lucky. I had an accident and cut my leg, but it didn't cut it completely off." It was so interesting to listen and follow the train of thought of these three boys.

Sixth Grade

Be on your guard; stand firm in the faith; be men of courage; be strong. Do everything in love.

I Corinthians 16:13-14

After the struggles of fifth grade, I knew sixth grade was going to be a challenge. Fifth grade had been our hardest year so far. As other children grew and matured, it seemed like the gap between Ross and other children was widening. As a parent, it is hard to stand back and watch this process. I just wanted to fix whatever was wrong and make my son's difficulties go away! I was so frustrated! It's like the feeling you get when you know a snow storm is coming and there is no place to take shelter. You just stand there, waiting for the snow to fall. As the first snowflake falls, the anxiety builds, but there is nothing you can do to prevent the coming storm. I don't know how many times I've felt the gnawing in the pit of my stomach or how many times my heart has ached. Seeing a child struggle, especially when it's your baby, is one of the hardest things a parent can go through. The helplessness I felt was overwhelming.

At the conclusion of fifth grade, there was a meeting at the sixth grade center to introduce parents to the protocol of the next year. The meeting was held in the gym of the sixth grade center. As parents hurried in from the May sunshine, I watched as many exchanged smiles with quick hand waves to their acquaintances. They looked as though they were comfortable in this setting and among friends. They looked like they belonged. Not me. As I sat there, I became painfully aware that I knew almost no one. After six years in the Owasso school system, I still felt as though it was my first year. I continued scanning the room for a familiar face. Finally, out of a gym filled with parents representing 600 new students, I found a familiar face—one I knew through my younger son.

Ms. Simons, the school counselor, began by saying, "Welcome to the Owasso Sixth Grade Center." I knew from previous experience that she and I would soon be up close and personal! That's just the way it seemed to go with me and school counselors. Ms. Simons gave out her direct phone number and I promptly wrote it down, knowing it would be a needed number for the future.

While other parents were chatting amongst themselves and discussing electives and whether their child would have first or second lunch, I sat there praying my son could handle the change. It all sounded like so much to handle. Children of this age were expected to drastically increase their level of personal responsibility. They would attend seven different 45-minute classes, and have a 30-minute lunch. The day began with an assembly every morning at 7:45 a.m., followed by classes beginning at 8:00 a.m. I was stunned by the thought of the school day beginning 7:45 a.m.! How would I manage that? Ross had never been one to go to bed early and being up and ready to get on the bus at 7:00 a.m. seemed almost impossible. I reassured myself it would just be a matter of adjustment. But I knew all too well that adjustments were never an easy task.

When Ross was in fifth grade, I gave a letter to each of his teachers during a parent teacher conference, listing the problems that Ross faced in the classroom. It also outlined the typical Aspergerian traits. I welcomed communication from the teachers, as I knew from experience that open lines of communication seemed to be the most effective means to keeping Ross up to speed in class. They looked over the letter and asked questions that let me know quickly that they knew very little about Asperger's Syndrome. It seems to me that we put our children and the teachers in precarious situations when we ask them to teach children who have challenges the teachers know so little about. There must be a way to get this information to the teachers so they can be more effective in the classroom, which will lead to greater success for our students. Maybe this belief is rooted in my naivety or a "save the world" personality, but I just think that increased knowledge could benefit both parties. It would benefit the other students in the classroom, too. It is no doubt that one child melting down in the classroom is a distraction to everyone. I can just see kids rolling their eyes and thinking, *Not him again!*

As Ross entered sixth grade, I again sent a letter to each of his teachers, similar to the letter I had provided his fifth grade teachers. I was determined to take a more proactive approach. I wanted to start the year off moving in the right direction. I wanted to build relationships that would foster an environment to help Ross be successful. The first week of school there was a "Meet the Teacher Night." Each teacher gave a 10-minute overview of classroom procedures and most included some personal information. I headed to the first class, wanting to make sure I introduced myself so the teacher could put a face to a name and establish the link of parent to child.

After the first session ended and the crowd had moved away from the teacher, I gave a smile as I extended my hand and said, "Hi, I'm Dee Phillips, Ross's mom." The teacher greeted me and then went on to say that a few of the kids from the class had made fun of Ross. She didn't say what for, but it didn't take much imagination for me to formulate a guess in my mind. She said she had asked Ross to leave the room, while she explained to the rest of the class that she wanted them to rally around Ross and help him. She said she would not tolerate the students making fun of him and that they needed to be kind to special needs children. As odd as it may be, this is the first time anyone had called Ross "special needs" to my face. Although I knew it was true, hearing it said out loud pierced me in some way. My heart sank. Once again, I hated the fact that things that come easy to others take every bit of strength Ross can muster to accomplish. I hate that he feels left out and is always the underdog. My stomach churns every time he deals with yet another obsessive compulsive routine. I just want him to fit in. I don't want him to be miserable. Why does he have to struggle so hard?

What School Is Like, in Ross's Words

I asked Ross when he was in sixth grade to describe to me what school was like and how he felt. This is what he said:

I feel like I'm in a race with school and me with OCD. And me as the turtle and my competitor is school, which is a cheetah. Make that a cheetah with a jet pack. I feel like I am two grades behind. I can advance my OCD and my control, but only as fast as a turtle can run. But the cheetah represented as the school and how fast school is going, by the time I'm in control of that semester, it's already another year. That's why it makes school so hard. I try even harder than last year to focus.

I feel that in school, people don't understand me that good, I'm misunderstood. As being a guy who's not regular, perhaps a medium amount of friends realize who I am really. I just have a disorder and I'm not that different. That's the reason I like them. A few people understand me and want to be around me. I'm glad to have friends like that. I just wish in the future that once in my lifetime I could be the turtle that beats the cheetah with the jetpack, just once! This year is harder because for some reason my OCD is harder to control. Teachers are not as understanding, some make it hard for me. It stacks up under pressure, even though I do half as much as most kids. It feels just as hard as doing all the homework of a normal kid. Conditions are different because there are a few teachers that are hard for me to keep up with, and it all stacks up and makes it harder for me. I'm just stacked up with the odds and it makes it hard with all the conditions I have.

Hitting Rock Bottom

In mid-November, I had the meeting with Ross's teachers that was described at the beginning of this book. That meeting left me knowing I had to do something. I had an appointment scheduled with Ross's developmental pediatrician the following week and I assured the teachers I understood their frustration and concern and would keep them up to date regarding the doctor's visit and communicate any necessary changes.

The next week, we had our appointment with Dr. Bloom. As usual, Ross was first to talk to Dr. Bloom. In just a few minutes, Ross was back in the waiting room and Dr. Bloom motioned me to his office. He explained that Ross was quite oppositional and argumentative, which was not really anything new, but usually Dr. Bloom could transition him into some productive dialogue. But not today. Ross was completely off track with the conversation, talking about things that were of no relevance, other than to display exactly how bad Ross's condition was. I explained to Dr. Bloom about the meeting I had had with the teachers the previous week and explained their concerns. I told him about Ross's increasing paranoia. I asked him about options and what we should do next. He said he thought we might be looking at adding a mood disorder diagnosis to the mix.

We had started occupational and physical therapy a couple of months prior to this visit with Dr. Bloom. The OT specialist was working with Ross on his dysgraphia and the PT specialist was working on his core strength. The sessions seemed to be getting us nowhere. Ross cried through the occupational therapy and curled up in a fetal position while doing physical therapy. At this point, I didn't know what to do. I felt like I was being aggressive in finding treatment, but the results seemed to be getting us nowhere. It all just served to give me a clearer picture of how bad things really were.

Since Ross's first breath, God has given me an abundance of patience and love for my child. For this, I thank Him every day. However, the frustration that I often feel can be overwhelming. Some days, every muscle in my body is tense from trying to keep myself together. There are times I want to lash out or scream or kick something or do all three. Until you have dealt with a child who is completely unreasonable, you probably don't understand how I feel. When Ross gets "stuck" there is no moving him! He can make the simplest task, a task you dread with all your might. He doesn't want to go to bed at night, and when he does, he can't sleep. Then he's tired so he doesn't want to get up in the morning. He has one speed, and that is slow. Rushing is not a talent of his. He doesn't want to take his medicine. He's picky about the kind of food he will eat. He only wants to wear certain clothes: jeans, a soft t-shirt, and Puma socks. If I don't help him gather up everything he needs for school, he'll leave his supplies at home. He won't eat at the cafeteria, he will just go without food. (The school actually called me and said they had to make him take a lunch, but he wouldn't eat any of it.) He doesn't want to do homework. He doesn't want to take a shower. He hates cleaning his room. Are you getting what I'm trying to communicate? There are no easy days!

CHAPTER ELEVEN

Seeing in Color

Dear friends, do not be surprised at the painful trial you are suffering, as though something strange were happening to you. But rejoice that you participate in the sufferings of Christ, so that you may be overjoyed when his glory is revealed.

1 PETER 4:12-13

The summer before Ross entered sixth grade, I read a book called *Change Your Brain, Change Your Life* by Dr. Daniel Amen. I was very intrigued by the book and shared some of the information with my sister. The book focused on the brain and showed photographs of SPECT scans that were done on people with a variety of disorders. It linked the problems of the brain to behavior issues. It discussed scans of people's brains who were faced with everything from head trauma to Alzheimer's. There was also some very valuable information about the chemicals that make the brain function normally and the effects that manifest themselves if there is an imbalance in those chemicals.

One day my sister called me and said, "You're not going to believe this. You know the book you talked to me about, *Change Your Brain, Change Your Life?* My Director of Nursing has a relative who took her son to one of the Amen Clinics in California. She said since that visit, he is doing better. Do you want me to get the information?" The first thing I could think was, *Absolutely, absolutely, absolutely!*

I made a call to Jennifer, the mother of the boy my sister had mentioned, as soon as I got the information. She was sweet and very helpful. She explained that the doctor her son had visited who performed the SPECT scan was actually an old friend of hers. They had attended college together. She commented that he is a great guy and that she thought he was opening a clinic in Dallas, Texas.

Jennifer said her son was doing better now. She mentioned how empowering it was to see what was actually going on in her son's brain. She also said it was a relief to know that his behavior was linked to a malfunction of the brain. This removed the guilt she had been carrying, as she wondered if she was just a bad parent. You know people think that if you just spank your child, you can control their behavior. If that worked with Ross, the child would have been cured at age three. Parents of children with ADHD and

Asperger's know how frustrating it is that many times, discipline yields little to no result.

The name of the doctor Jennifer's son had seen was Dr. Todd Clements. I researched as much information as I could find about Dr. Clements. I was especially impressed with the fact that he was a Christian. In addition to having a list of impressive credentials in child psychiatry, he was also a youth pastor. Jennifer had given me Dr. Clements' email address. I emailed him and awaited a response.

Bright and early on Monday morning, I received a response. Dr. Clements confirmed that he had just opened a clinic in Dallas and said he would have his assistant give me a call and share some information with me. I was elated. There was something stirring inside of me. I knew that God was behind the scenes working things out for me. A renewed sense of hope filled my mind. At last I would see what was really going on with Ross. I would have something tangible. Not just speculation or a guess or an answer to appease me for a moment, but something I could see. I had spent twelve years wondering what was really going on inside his head, twelve years of blaming myself, twelve years of trying to hold it together while others dished out criticism and disgust. Now, I was finally going to get to see!

I received a phone call from Lynda at the Clements Clinic. She did an excellent job explaining the process and lending an ear as I vented in moments of frustration and helplessness. She said I was going to need to fill out an evaluation form that was over twenty pages long. She also said that Ross was going to need to come off his medication before the scan and the consultation with the doctor. It took a moment for that to sink in...Ross, off his medication. Ross had been on meds since he was five. I wondered what he would be like without the medications. Part of me wondered if I was really up for the challenge. All I could think was *Sweet Jesus, You're going to have to help me on this one.* I was not at all interested in doing this one solo.

I scheduled the scan for the end of Christmas break so I could take Ross off his meds while he wasn't in school. Removing the meds from Ross's system had to be a gradual process. I just kept reminding myself that whatever we faced, it would be worth it in the end. I read positive affirmations over and over and quoted my favorite scriptures. I knew I was entering uncharted territory and a strong spirit and mind would be essential for a successful outcome! You may be thinking that I was a little dramatic about this whole thing. Let me assure you I was not. It was going to be an extremely difficult time.

My mom scheduled a flight and met me in Dallas. I was so grateful to have the support of a family member, but I'm not sure my mom really knew what she was signing up for. Simple words can't adequately describe Ross's behavior. Oh, my sweet mother of pearl. It was like a scene from the movie, *Tommy Boy,* when Tommy and his partner are on a road trip to sell car parts to save the family company from collapse. On the way, they hit a deer in the road. They feel so bad for the deer, they pick it up and put it in the back seat of the car to take and dispose of it properly. As they travel down the road, Tommy looks in the review mirror only to see bright eyes and antlers starring back at him. The deer was not dead, but alive and now trapped in the back-seat of a car traveling down the highway. The trapped deer freaks out, completely destroying the car and its convertible top as he makes his exit. Ross was like the trapped deer—WILD!

I cannot articulate the degree to which Ross was out of control. He wasn't taking his sleep medication, and he literally went days with little or no sleep. At the Clements Clinic, he was beating his head against the wall. He put his head in the middle of a chair and was spinning around in a circle. He was opening and slamming the door into the clinic. I was literally following him around, trying to keep him from doing something he wasn't supposed to do. He would talk loudly and go on and on about a subject, even more than normal. As people in the clinic looked at me, I just smiled and apologized for his disruption. (I'm sure they were thinking it was a good idea I was seeking help!) I was somewhat embarrassed, although the degree of embarrassment wasn't nearly as severe as it was years ago. I guess I have grown thicker skin.

I tried taking Ross to see a movie, as watching movies has always been one of his favorite things, but he couldn't sit still long enough to watch. He was moving side to side in his chair, making noise, and kept asking me questions (not quietly, I might add). We ended up leaving early, and I was quite frustrated. *Can't you just sit still for a little while,* I thought. Ross wasn't just mildly irritated, he was in complete chaos.

The first day at the clinic, we answered a lot of questions and provided pages of information about Ross's behavior since birth. They asked extensive questions about Ross's father and me. Ross also received his first scan. While he was in a dimly lit room, the nurse put an IV in for a certain amount of time to allow Ross to get accustomed to his surroundings and relax a bit and then they performed the scan while he was resting. Even then, performing the scan was a challenge because Ross had great difficulty laying still. The technician repeatedly told him to lie still to ensure the greatest accuracy in reading the scans.

The second day at the clinic was more intense. Ross has a phobia about needles, so going back for the second IV was not going to happen without a fight. When we got up that morning, he informed me we were not going back for a second scan. He had rethought things and "he liked his uniqueness." I told him I liked his uniqueness too, but informed him that we WERE going to have a second scan unless there was some act of God or nature that prevented me from carrying him inside the clinic.

He didn't really like that answer. When it came time for the IV, he actually tried to escape out of the clinic. Not to worry, I was prepared and on heightened alert.

The second scan was performed when Ross was concentrating on the Connor's Continuous Performance Task, a 15-minute computerized test of attention. As soon as we finished the second scan, the first thing Ross asked for was his medicine. He stated, "I'm tired of being a raging maniac." It was only a couple of hours after taking his meds, that he settled down and was able to control himself more appropriately. This experience helped me realize that although we were still having severe problems, the medications that he was currently taking were more of an asset than I had realized!

Meeting with Dr. Clements

We met with Dr. Clements to discuss the results of the SPECT scans. Most of that meeting was a fog to me. Maybe this was because of my lack of sleep or maybe it was from the shock I felt when I saw Ross's brain scan compared to a scan of a normal brain of a child his age. The scans were color-coded making it easy to observe the differences. The color-coding related to the activity of the brain. White was the most active, followed by red, and then blue indicated the least activity. It only took one look to see that Ross's brain had a significantly greater amount of white and red areas than it was supposed to have.

Dr. Clements started our meeting by saying Ross is a very complex young man. This comment was starting to be universal among his doctors. He went over the findings of the scan. I didn't realize at the time, exactly what he was communicating. My mind seemed to be stuck on the image generated by the scan. In a sense, I was relieved—relieved that there was a physical reason for Ross's behavior. Another part of me mourned because of the challenges he would face the rest of his life. But I reminded myself that knowledge is power. The fact that we now had more information about Ross's disorders, made us more equipped to deal with the problems.

The SPECT scan showed what they called a "Ring of Fire" pattern in Ross's brain. When present, this pattern may be associated with mood issues, cognitive inflexibility, sensitivity to the environment, difficulty with transitions, anxiety and irritability. In some people, this pattern may be related to bipolar disorder, a diffuse inflammatory process, allergies that affect the brain, or some form of prior toxic exposure. Individuals with this finding often receive clinical diagnoses of ADHD, but tend to respond incompletely to ADHD meds. Symptoms associated with this pattern include mood dyscontrol, oppositional behavior, aggression, cognitive inflexibility, sensitivity to the environment, and difficulty with transitions.

Second, the SPECT scan showed evidence of increased tracer activity in the anterior cingulate gyrus. Dr. Clements explained that this is often associated with problems shifting attention, which is manifested by a combination of symptoms such as cognitive inflexibility, obsessive thoughts, compulsive behaviors, excessive worrying, argumentativeness, and oppositional behavior of "getting stuck" on certain thoughts or actions. This is often seen in people with obsessive-compulsive disorders, oppositional defiant disorders, eating disorders, addictive disorders, anxiety disorders, Gilles de la Tourette's and chronic pain.

Third, the scan showed increased left and right parietal lobe tracer activity. This finding is often associated with hypersensitivity to light, noise, touch and other issues in the environment. This problem is also implicated in attentional issues.

The scan showed activity that would explain Ross's anxiety issues. It also showed activity that would explain his mood disorders, impulsivity, short attention span, distractibility and difficulties with organization and planning. Dr. Clements explained that the cerebellum is the most intensely active structure on the SPECT scan of a healthy individual. Ross's SPECT scan showed decreased activity in this area of his brain. There is growing literature describing behavioral disturbances associated with abnormalities of the cerebellar structure or function. The research seems to support the belief that the cerebellum is involved in coordinating higher-order processes such as planning and impulse control and other complex behaviors because it is known to send projections to various regions of the cerebral cortex, especially the frontal and prefrontal cortices. The decreased activity in the cerebellar structure of Ross's brain would explain his inability to control himself and his moods.

Finally, the SPECT scan showed increased left and right temporal lobe tracer activity, especially on the scan when Ross was to be at rest.

Dr. Clements explained that this abnormality may be associated with several different symptoms including mood instability, irritability, memory problems, abnormal perceptions (auditory or visual illusions, periods of déjà vu), periods of anxiety and irritability with little provocation, periods of "spaciness" or confusion, and unexplained headaches or abdominal pain. Problems with the right temporal lobe have been associated with social withdrawal, social skills struggles and depression.

I remember Dr. Clements stating that physically, Ross was just not able to perform many of the daily tasks that were asked of him without great stress and anxiety. This was something he simply couldn't help. It was a relief to know that many of his behaviors were a function of brain development, and not a function of defiance. It has always been a battle for me to try to distinguish behaviors that he could control and those that he could not.

We ended the meeting with a list of things to do. We were going to change some of his prescription medications and we were going to introduce some vitamin and mineral supplements into his regimine. It was stressed that Ross needed regular physical activity, and that this activity would aid in his progress toward improvement. I left the meeting with a renewed sense of hope and a course to pursue from this point.

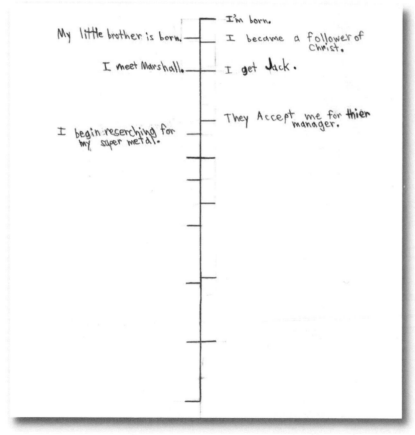

Ross made this timeline when he was age 11.
Even at a young age, he knew the value of following Christ!

Name _____ Ross

WHEN I'M GROWN-UP

I will be honest.

Do grown-ups drive you crazy?
Well, you will be one yourself soon.
What will you be like then?

I hope I **will** be:

1. I hope I will be a dad with a lovely cute.
2. I hope I will be teaching my kids about the lord.
3. I hope I go to heven.
4. I hope I will be hansom.
5. I hope I will be having a cute dog
6. I hope I will be funny.
7. I hope I will be helthy.

I hope I will **not** be:

1. I hope I will not be going to hell.
2. I hope I will not be a bad guy.
3. I hope I will not be a drug user.
4. I hope I will not have kiss that use drugs.
5. I hope I will not be ssiying bad words.
6. I hope I will not be evel.
7. I hope I will not be a couch petato.

Ross wrote this when he was in elementary school.
He outlines what he hopes for when he grows up.

CHAPTER TWELVE

Seventh Grade: A Turn Around

"Whoever humbles himself like this child is the greatest in the kingdom of heaven. And whoever welcomes a little child like this in my name welcomes me."

MATTHEW 18:4-5

Town and Country School (Fall 2009)

At the end of sixth grade, I knew we had to look into other schooling options for Ross. What we were doing was clearly not working, but what to do was always the daunting question. We had completed the SPECT scan, which clearly showed we had a problem. Since our meeting with Dr. Clements, we had seen improvement, but Ross was still so volatile. He could be happy one minute and the next you would see his lip quiver as he fought back tears. He clearly was unhappy.

One day, close to the end of Ross's sixth grade year, I stopped by the school to take Ross a couple of gifts to give to his favorite teachers for Teacher Appreciation Day. He was sitting in the hall by the library, away from the noise of the cafeteria. With six hundred plus sixth graders at this school, the noise and the hustle and bustle of changing classes bothered me, so I can only imagine what it felt like to Ross. He was sitting on the floor away from the others, with his shoulders slumped forward and his head down. When I looked at him, he had tears streaming down his face. "Why can't I just fit in, Mom?" I encouraged him, as moms do, but deep inside I ached. To see a child struggle, puts a pit in your stomach. To see others be so cruel to my son, made me angry. I just wanted to take him and run away.

So we began looking into other options for schooling. Home schooling wasn't an option. Ross fought me so hard to complete one simple paper, crying for thirty minutes about a paper that would only take five minutes to complete, that the thought of fighting all day, every day, wasn't something I thought would be beneficial for either one of us.

Our research led us to a school that was primarily for children with ADD and Asperger's. It was located over thirty miles away from where we lived. There was a rather lengthy enrollment process, as they wanted to make sure that each student was a right fit for the school. It was a private school, so therefore sending Ross there would require a rather substantial financial investment as well.

We went to an interview in June to meet with the director of the school. She interviewed Ross and asked several questions. As we walked through the school, I didn't note anything that was particularly special. The campus was composed of rather old buildings. However, those I talked to who had students who attended the school, seemed to give a rather majestic description of it. When we finished the interview, the director said she would review the information and let us know if Ross would be a good fit. Later that summer, we were contacted and welcomed to the new school. I was so hopeful this was an answer to prayer.

Starting a New School

The first few weeks at the new school didn't go so well. Ross refused to walk from building to building because of his paranoia of wasps. At times, it took three teachers to coax him to go outside. He refused to go outside during a fire drill, because he knew it was only a drill and he already knew how to exit the building. He stated, "What a complete waste of time."

He stood firm on his principle that schoolwork was a waste of time. He needed to complete his research in order to save the world!

Ms. Etier, the school principal, called me several times to discuss the problems Ross was having at school. During her fourth phone call to me, she said that she didn't know if the school was equipped to deal with a child whose condition was quite as severe as Ross's. She said that maybe the scope of his disorders were beyond what they could accommodate.

I felt so frustrated, felt such a deep mourning. The hurt was so bad. I had been so hopeful that this new school would help with the problems we were having. We had exhausted most of our resources, and had made a major time and financial commitment in the hope that this school would provide a solution.

To her credit, Ms. Etier did not give up on Ross. She quickly adjusted his schedule and provided solutions to help make his day more tolerable. This was a major difference from our experience with the public school system. She shorted his school hours to half a day. She provided Ross with a "wasp band" that he wore on his wrist to keep wasps away while he was at recess. She gave him permission to go to her office when he was feeling overwhelmed. She allowed him to call me if he felt it was necessary. In all of this, her goal was to keep him at school and engaged as long as possible. She spent time on the phone with me, discussing Ross's behaviors and listening to the feedback I gave her about past experiences. I felt like I was being heard!

I notified Ross's developmental pediatrician of the problems he was continuing to have at school. He reviewed his file and the information from The Clements Clinic. He felt that based on Ross's behavior and the information from his SPECT scan, we needed to make some adjustments to Ross's medications.

Soon after the change in medication, Ross commented that he was able to go outside without his "wasp band" and was not afraid of wasps as much as he had been. He took our dog out for a walk by himself without his bracelet. He reported, "no tears at school." He did, however, say he got frustrated when he couldn't get the teeth correct on a dinosaur that he was drawing during free time. Overall, his stress level seemed much better. I talked to the principal about his progress. She said, "He is like a different child."

At home, Ross's behavior was improving as well. He seemed to have fewer meltdowns. He laughed more. He transitioned between tasks with greater ease. He had a greater use of his executive function and was thinking ahead more.

SPD (Sensory Processing Disorder)

I cannot stress enough how much the work of Ross's occupational therapist, Judy McCarter, contributed to his success. She provided a great deal of information to help us understand Asperger's Syndrome Disorder, especially in the area of sensory processing disorder.

According to Judy, Dr. Jean Ayres is a pioneer in the field of study of sensory processing disorders. Dr. Ayers defines sensory integration as the neurological process by which sensations are organized and become meaningful. The sensations come by way of auditory, visual, tactile, gustatory, olfactory, vestibular and proprioceptive input. Sensory integration dysfunction occurs when an individual has difficulty interpreting the sensations from the body. An example of this would be walking outside when it was cold but having your body not detect that the temperature was cold.

Sensory processing occurs when the nervous system interprets information from the sensory systems and is able to develop meaningful responses to that information. An example of proper sensory processing would be walking outside when it was cold, being able to process that feeling of being cold and then putting on a coat to warm yourself. Sensory regulation occurs when an individual is able to maintain a calm and focused state in the face of sensory processing.

The study of sensory processing disorders is personal for Judy McCarter, as this is something she admits she struggled with throughout her childhood. It is what drove her to become an occupational therapist, so that she could learn more about this disorder that can seem so subtle to the casual observer, but can be so debilitating to the one suffering from it, causing fear, uncertainty, decreased self-esteem and decreased self-confidence. On the outside, a person suffering from sensory processing disorders might just appear to be clumsy, apathetic, unmotivated, sloppy, disorganized and not engaged with what is going on in the moment. But on the inside, SPD sufferers are actually fearful, anxious, apprehensive, uncertain and feel like their life is not predictable and that that they have little ability to control anything. These internal feelings are what causes SPD sufferers to react to things they way they do. For example, when something smells too strong or offensive, a SPD sufferer might flee the room and refuse to go back in. It is hard for people without SPD to understand these actions because they can't see, hear, smell or feel the sensations like someone with SPD does.

Think of this hypersensitivity like Superman's X-ray vision. Since individuals with SPD interpret sensory information differently, their perceptions of this sensory information might also be different. Just because we do not interpret things in the same way does not mean that we should not acknowledge that someone else's interpretation is just as real to them. The key is to embrace our differences and our different perspectives. Someone observing a person with a sensory processing disorder may think that they over-react or underreact to their environmental input. The reality is, many people with sensory processing disorders don't feel comfortable in their own skin. Their body feels a little bit "off".

For someone with SPD, their ability to process information can change multiple times within a given day, depending on how irritated their nervous system is from different types of sensory input, how much anxiety or anticipatory anxiety they are dealing with, or how many unpredictable changes have occurred in a given time period. Individuals with sensory processing disorder can improve through treatment and training in strategic compensation. This was the case with Ross. One day, Judy McCarter witnessed Ross standing under a covered picnic area at Town and Country School. He was spinning around, waving his arms and screeching, "Get away wasps!" Judy could tell that Ross wasn't scared—he was terrified. His sense of fear was strong and powerful and it was controlling his ability to function.

When Judy asked the principal about Ross's fears, she said that three teachers had to escort him between buildings to, as Ross put it, help protect him from the wasps. Judy suggested putting some kind of bug deterrent onto Ross to keep the wasps away, such as a sonic device that would emit sonic sounds. The principal purchased a bug band and put it on Ross. That allowed him to travel between buildings without fear.

Over time, Ross and Judy became fast friends and still share a certain kinship with being over responsive or under responsive to sensory stimuli. They both share compromised processing with their vestibular system, which can cause them to become dizzy or sick with movement such as riding in a car. Ross has difficulty tolerating different textures, crowds and people being too close to him, and he doesn't like to be touched when he is not prepared for the touch. After all of their time together, Judy gave this description of Ross:

He is a funny, engaging, sympathetic and delightful young adult. Ross is extremely intuitive and sensitive and has a remarkable ability to produce visual arts and graphics. He continually amazes me with his insight into the way he processes sensory information. Ross is learning strategies to change his sensory regulation to provide tools for life which will help him understand the unique way he integrates his sensory information. It has been a blessing for me to have the opportunity to work with Ross. His individualistic perception is a gift that allows him to be his unique person with his special gifts and talents. It is a joy for me to work with a young man who can verbally articulate how his body is interpreting his sensory information. Ross is a teacher to me and helps me understand different ways that sensory information can be interpreted. He always looks forward to going to therapy or as he calls it "The Fun House."

Meeting the Principal

Later in the school year, I set up a meeting with Ms. Etier, the Upper School Principal. I wanted to discuss

Ross's progress and learn more about the school. She began our meeting by emphasizing that no two students are alike at Town and Country School. This is actually one of her favorite things about the school. The students are all so unique and possess wonderfully great talents and abilities. Although two students may have the same diagnoses, how those behaviors are manifested differ for each child. She stated that with Asperger's Syndrome, OCD is the most common co-morbid disorder that she has experienced. She said a student will often focus or "obsess" about one thing.

In light of these facts, she said the school strives to make each student feel comfortable and to help students transition from one task to another. How each student responds is as different as the students them-selves. Many need visual stimulation to help aid in the process. Teachers are trained on the principles of "Love and Logic."

Ms. Etier said one of the biggest frustrations in her job comes from parents. Some parents are truly wonderful and are realistic about situations, their children, and their abilities. However, that is not the general rule for all. Some parents enable their children, defending and rescuing when it isn't really necessary. The philosophy of Town and Country School is that children need to stand up and experience natural events and consequences and be left to navigate things on their own sometimes, even if they fail. They want their students to be free to learn certain lessons when there is a safety net to catch them. To this end, the students are empowered to make choices for themselves. When you give them choices, it empowers them and usually the struggle diminishes. As to the success of Asperger's students, they have found that once they are engaged in a lesson, they are usually good students.

One of the most profound things Ms. Etier told me that day was that many teachers judge their success by their ability to control students. She stressed that what a teacher must realize is that controlling students is not the key to being a good teacher. The same principle can be applied to parenting. Just because you can't control your child, it doesn't mean you're not a good parent. If I've learned nothing else, I've learned that when you have a child who has disorders, all the planning and coaching in the world can't stop a meltdown.

Once Ms. Etier briefed me on the overall philosophy and organization of the school, the subject of our conversation then transitioned to Ross specifically. She stated Ross is the first student she has had at the school who is dealing with more than just Asperger's Syndrome or ADD. She said usually the students at the school struggle with the social side of school, like making friends or talking about a specific topic too much, but they don't have too many problems in the classroom.

With Ross's multiple diagnoses, Ms. Etier said she couldn't believe he made it through public school as long as he had. She said the number one complaint she hears most from parents who come to Town and

Country is that, in the public school system, children cannot get the specialized services they need, as all students are treated the same. The most rewarding part of her job is finding solutions for these children when before, others thought there was no hope.

In Ms. Etier's opinion, Ross's anxiety is the most debilitating of his illnesses. Transition is hard for him. With transition, comes anxiety. She witnessed Ross having cycling conversations in his head. He would tell himself he can't do it and would get himself all worked up before he even tried the new task. In his mind, he would convince himself that he can't do it and therefore, the anxiety is there before the new task even begins. She said this wasn't intentional, he just genuinely couldn't get a thought out of his head. When he gets stuck on a thought or an obsession, no amount of reasoning will change his mind!

She noticed that Ross also experiences more grandiose ideas and more of a "save the world" mentality than most of those with Asperger's. She stated she usually doesn't experience the "loss of reality" with most of her other students like she does with Ross.

Even with all of this, the meeting ended on a positive note. Despite all the issues Ross was facing, Ms. Etier said he was one of her most improved students since the beginning of year. I took comfort in the fact that we were seeing progress.

After I met with Ms. Etier, I thought back to our conversation many times. The two things Ms. Etier said that day that made the greatest impression on me were her confirmation that Ross really is a complex individual and her assertion that controlling students isn't the definition of a good teacher, nor is it the definition of a good parent. I'm not advocating doing away with discipline, but if you have a child like Ross and discipline doesn't seem to be a deterrent, it doesn't mean you are a failure as a parent.

I thought long and hard about the issue of control. Before I had Ross, I believed that a good parent was one who could control her children. She would "cut the look" or snap her fingers and the children would obey her requests.

What was revealed to me was that control of others is not a fruit of the Spirit. Nowhere in the Bible have I found that the fruitfulness of God's work in our lives is manifested in our ability to control others! No, we show our fruit by how we relate to our circumstances. Do we exhibit self-control, long suffering, peace and joy? These are evidence of the fruit of the Spirit. What a revelation this was! I cannot control the disorders my son has. I cannot control the reaction that he has to various situations. The only thing that I can control is me. Therefore my success as a parent and as a follower of God cannot be defined by my ability to control my son. What a relief!

14:31

Fourteen minutes and thirty-one seconds I spent on the phone listening to Ross clearly in "stress mode" over an inside recess at school. It was December and cold outside. The school was having an inside recess as opposed to going outside. Ross was upset for several reasons. First, he likes outside recess because he likes to swing. For him, this is a calming mechanism that helps him prepare for the rest of the day. Secondly, he had nothing to do while at inside recess. Just "hanging" with friends was a foreign concept. He needs to be engaged with an activity and idle time has never been a friend of his. Lastly, we had just returned from a vacation to see my family in New Mexico. The long ride in the car and disruption in routine, made him irritable and less flexible than normal. He wanted me to come and pick him up. He was sure a ride home with me and some time doing his favorite things would cheer him up.

The principal had given Ross the option to sit in her office during inside recess and draw or read books, since that's something he usually enjoys. But today, he was locked in a loop! No amount of reasoning was going to change his mind. So I listened patiently. Over and over he told me all the reasons why the principal's option would not work and how I needed to find another alternative for him. Ross was recalcitrant. I reinforced the principal's decision and stated that she was his authority figure and that he had to follow her instructions. Ross replied, "You are my authority figure and I need you to fix this!" Again, I explained his options and said I would see him at two o'clock.

These sorts of conversations always have me swinging the pendulum in my mind as to the best way to handle Ross. I know how difficult school is for him. Interacting with others and the everyday routine demands are very taxing for him. He is literally drained by the time he gets home. He doesn't want to go anywhere or do much of anything. He likes to settle in on the History Channel, draw, or watch a movie he's seen numerous times. Expecting much more out of him will result in a letdown. He is spent! But the other part of me wants to teach him to problem solve. If he continually escapes his problems, running from the unpleasant feelings, then we will stall progress and his development. I stood firm on my decision to leave him at school. He was able to transition and finish the rest of the day.

Ross completed the year on a successful note. He made friends and, equally as important, he liked going to school. I talked to his teachers at the end of his school year and they all commented on his progress. I received an email from his math teacher the last week of school. Ross took a math test at the beginning of the year. He retook the same test in the spring. His math score almost doubled. Not only was he enjoying school more, he was progressing academically as well.

Keep Your Circle Open

At the end of the school year, we traveled to Texas and New Mexico to visit family. On the way home, I commented to Ross that he had good behavior and I was proud of him. He said he was trying to learn to keep his "circle open." I asked him what he meant by that. He said when your circle is closed, you are not willing to look at your options. If your circle is open, then you look at your options and are more willing to adapt. I liked this analogy. Better yet, I was impressed that he "got it." Now when I am feeling overwhelmed, I remind myself to "keep my circle open."

Ross is now 14 years old. When not at school, he fills his days researching ways to explore the universe. He transports mechanical pencils, a protractor, a ruler and paper most everywhere he goes. He still loves watching television. Science channels are his favorite.

10-27-09

Ross P.

Deadra owe Deadra.
She's as sweet as candy
and as lovible as a puppy.
She's as beautiful as a
flower. She's as cool as the
North Pole and as hot as the
Sun.

Ross wrote this poem for me when he was in seventh grade.

CHAPTER THIRTEEN

A Heart Reborn

Dear brothers, is your life full of difficulties and temptations? Then be happy, for when the way is rough, your patience has a chance to grow. So let it grow, and don't try to squirm out of your problems. For when your patience is in full bloom, then you will be ready for anything, strong in character, full and complete.

JAMES 1:2-5 TLB

Webster's New World Dictionary defines *change* as "to put or take a thing in place of something else; to make different." Sometimes we experience change in unlikely places. Sometimes change comes about through pain.

Because of what I have experienced in my life as I've raised my son, I am a changed person. I am a better person. I am so thankful that I have been given the opportunity to live deeper. I now have a compassionate heart and a tender spirit. I have eyes that see others' pain. The growth I have experienced is not something you can buy. My shallow self and critical spirit are starting to vanish. I have a greater acceptance of others and respect for their differences. I now appreciate and can see that God has created us all, although not all the same. Consider these words God inspired Paul to write:

> For I wish that all men were even as I myself. But each one has his own gift from God, one in this manner and another in that.
>
> I CORINTHIANS 7:7 NKJV

> Having then gifts differing according to the grace that is given to us, let us use them: if prophecy, let us prophesy in proportion to our faith.
>
> ROMANS 12:6 NKJV

God clearly states in His Word that He has created us all different, so why is being different such a problem? I wish I could answer that question eloquently and with academic finesse, but I can't. However, the best way to approach these differences is what we, as parents, have to learn and teach our children.

I Am Not Skilled to Understand

One Sunday morning at church, the congregation sang a song that really made an impression on me. It went like this....

I am not skilled to understand

What God has willed, what God has planned

I only know at His right hand

Stands One who is my Savior...

(Aaron Shust, "My Savior, My God."

Copyright © 2006 by Bridge Building Music)

Those four lines spoke volumes to me. When we go through a crisis, we seek answers, looking for something to give us hope.

We have to decide to accept God's sovereignty.

I will never know the reasons why I face the challenges in my life that I face. I just know, there is a purpose.

No matter how much effort we put into trying to figure out why something has happened to us, there often is no clear answer. We search for hours wondering "why me" and asking how I can possibly be deserving of these circumstances. We may actually spend most of our lives regretting the choices we've made or simply complaining about our situation. We're frustrated that life isn't going the way we had it planned in our mind. We want immediate gratification and patience is a virtue we seem to overlook. We look for a quick fix or at least something that will make us feel better.

Reasoning doesn't provide us with answers, either. We look around at the proverbial "Neighbor" who looks to have it so much easier and better than we do. We often fall into a pit of emotions, feeling helpless and exhausted. We become victims of our "unfair circumstances." We bathe in self-pity and excuses. Our "why me" attitude spills over to all areas of our life, leaving us dealing with problems in our personal relationships, careers and with ourselves.

When we go through a trial, it is in these times that we must challenge our present state of being and hopefully learn and grow from our experience. We may believe that we are the ones who need to help others, when in actuality, we may be the ones with the most to learn.

Learning Is a Process

I know how to be abased, and I know how to abound. Everywhere and in all things I have learned both to be full and to be hungry, both to abound and to suffer need.

PHILIPPIANS 4:12 NKJV

To learn... what does that mean? It means that whatever knowledge we have, we are not born with it. Only by experience and maturity do we learn. Learning is an action. In the same way, it's not our circumstances that determine our character, it's our response to those circumstances that defines us!

Paul, Peter and the other apostles learned the secret of developing an eternal perspective in the midst of earthly problems. They were able to live above their circumstances and rejoice, even while being persecuted, because they had a firm grasp of who they were in Christ and where they were going.

What Ross Has Taught Me About Life

I've learned that life extends beyond "me." I need to be always looking for what I can do to help other people.

I've learned my patience can extend beyond what I thought was possible.

I've learned that no matter how difficult things are, we have to be persistent and not give up. We have to never quit pushing for progress.

I've learned to have a fresh perspective on life and to accept those different from myself.

I've learned that God is always working in my life, whether I see it or not.

I've learned that challenges make us stronger.

I've learned to be more flexible. Things don't always have to be done a certain way, and it's okay.

I've learned to be less critical. There may be circumstances beyond what the eye can see.

I've learned not to worry about the criticism of others, as long as I am true to my own convictions.

I've learned that true satisfaction in life comes from helping others.

I've learned that no matter how hard I try, I can never change someone else.

I've learned God doesn't operate on my timeline.

I have learned I will never be happy if I let circumstances dictate my happiness.

Most of all, I've learned how to feel the deepest love possible!

What I Love About Ross

I love laying on the bed with Ross and watching the movies he likes as he says, "Watch this part Mom, isn't it great?" like it's the first time I've ever seen it.

I love going to Barnes and Noble with Ross and watching him browse through books for hours.

I love listening to the honesty that rolls from Ross's lips and knowing where I stand with him. With him, there are no hidden agendas or false pretenses.

I love watching Ross interact with animals, seeing his gentleness and connection to them.

I love Ross's acceptance of others and his genuine nature.

I love watching Ross draw, seeing his brilliance come alive from the tip of a pencil.

I love how Ross admits his faults so openly.

I love Ross's sense of humor and at the same time, his cluelessness when it comes to jokes.

I love the way Ross lives "out of the box." It's so refreshing for a Type A personality.

I love Ross for who he is. I would never want him to be anything else.

In Conclusion...

Experience produces relative perceptions. Once you face something that is beyond your control, that you cannot fix no matter how hard you try, it is then that you develop humility. Your purpose in life shifts, or at least mine did. My experience has led to a desire to help others. I had always been performance driven until I gave birth to Ross. Through him, I learned I don't have to perform to be accepted. I am okay with being a mom and loving my child.

I have learned the full measure of what is contained in these three words: patience, endurance and faith. Isn't this what Christ asks of us? Even though we don't understand the obstacles of life, He asks that we be patient. And when the answer is not readily available, He asks us to endure and keep the faith as we face whatever challenges are in our path. I've taken much solace in these words written by Paul:

Because the foolishness of God is wiser than men, and the weakness of God is stronger than men. For you see your calling, brethren, that not many wise according to the flesh, not many mighty, not many noble, are called. But God has chosen the foolish things of the world to put to shame the wise, and God has chosen the weak things of the world to put to shame the things which are mighty; and the base things of the world and the things that are despised God has chosen, and the things which are not, to bring to nothing the things that are, that no flesh should glory in His presence.

1 CORINTHIANS 25-29 NKJV

As you come to the close of this book, I wish I could be there to give you a hug. The expressions on our faces would testify to each other silently, without saying a word, the deep emotion that is part of raising a child with a disorder. I know you understand as I do, that the complete sorrow, frustration, and fear that we feel can be overwhelming. I hope that by sharing my story, I have touched a part of your soul, a part that can only be reached by someone with a similar experience.

I know you are exhausted. Maybe it's from holding your breath as you watch your child break every social rule known to man, or from trying to get your child to stop talking as he engages once again in a monologue about the biggest dinosaur, with an adult who clearly has no interest in what your child has to say. Or maybe your exhaustion stems from the intense anguish you feel when you see other children walking away from your child, rolling their eyes and snickering as your child stands there broken. Maybe the exhaustion comes from frustration as you address the same issues over and over while seeing no improvement. Maybe the fatigue stems from jumping through every hurdle to keep the peace, only to realize there is no peace. Maybe it stems from listening to your child sob uncontrollably as they describe how they just want one friend. Maybe you're exhausted from watching your child melt down over a seemingly trivial issue in public in front of those "perfect parents" who give you "the eye" with laser speed (I know you know the look!), or say to you, "My child never behaves that way."

Maybe your exhaustion stems from listening as your child tells your best friend how dirty her bathroom is. Maybe the exhaustion is a result of the fear we feel when we hear the daunting news, "We don't know what causes your child's problems and, well, there is no cure."

Hope—isn't that all we really want? Hope that better days are ahead and that the struggles that our child faces will vanish and that one day, the overwhelming feelings will dissipate. We have given up on finding a miraculous cure and now hope is what keeps us going. Sometimes all you need to find that hope is just someone to tell you it can and will get better.

Winning Endurance

You have to make up your mind! As a parent of a child with a disorder, you have to make up your mind to persevere. You have to have tenacity, because you will be tried over and over again. Take heart as you read these words from God written just for you.

He who earnestly seeks good finds favor.

PROVERBS 11:27 NKJV

Anxiety in the heart of man causes depression, but a good word makes it glad.

PROVERBS 12:25 NKJV

And do not be conformed to this world, but be transformed by the renewing of your mind, that you may prove what is that good and acceptable and perfect will of God.

ROMANS 12:2 NKJV

The things which you learned and received and heard and saw in me, these do, and the God of peace will be with you.

PHILIPPIANS 4:9 NKJV

CHAPTER FOURTEEN

Ross's Classics

As any parent knows, there are moments in your child's life that will remain in your memory forever. I wanted to share with you some of Ross's classic moments.

Age 5:

Ross had Ms. Shade in K-4. Ms. Shade must have been a very special teacher, as this was Ross's comment when he saw Ms. Shade: "When I see Ms. Shade, she makes my heart glow."

Age 9:

We had a red bird that kept flying into our window. Ross said, "You flying Red Bird of Death, quit hitting our window!"

Age 10:

Ross: "Grandma, will you cut up my cinnamon roll?"

Grandma: "Ross, I'm sure you can do it."

Ross: "But Grandma, I don't want to. It's a waste of time. I'm sure it will take me six or five minutes. I could be watching TV during that time."

Age 11:

The nurse at the pediatrician's office asked if Ross had had any major illnesses or surgeries, to which I replied "No." Ross said, "Excuse me, but I just was sick last week and it was torture to my buttocks." Later, when they checked his private area, he turned to me and said, "Oh, isn't this lovely."

One day, Ross said to me, "Mom, you look beautiful." I replied, "Why, thank you, Ross." Then he continued, "But, not so good when you wake up in the morning. But after you put your make-up on and do your hair and wear that one black shirt, then you look beautiful."

One day, Ross went off on his inability to ride a bike: "Why can't I ride a bike? It's not fair. Why can't I ride a bike? I've been doing this for ten or nine days and I still can't do this. Rhett can do it and he's four years younger than me. It's not fair." The truth is, Ross couldn't really care less if he rides a bike. He would rather be inside watching the Science Channel and building something with Legos. To him, sports are boring and a waste of time and he doesn't understand why anyone would want to exert that much energy!

Ross's reflection on getting old: "I don't want to get older because I don't want to get two chins."

Age 12:

This dialogue took place one day while Ross was at the table, eating.

Ross: *Burp*

Me: "Ross, don't burp like that. And say excuse me."

Ross: "Well, I had to burp; if I keep it in, it will turn to a fart."

Me: "Honey, don't say fart at the table."

Ross: "Why? What do you want me to say? A giant bubble coming out my behind?"

I tried to prepare and coach Ross before social situations in which I knew someone was going to be present with a situation or condition I did not want him to discuss. Ross lacked any sense of social decorum. In one instance, a friend and his girlfriend were coming over for dinner. The friend had lost his eye in an accident and had an artificial eye, which was very obvious. I explained to Ross that even though something is obvious, it doesn't mean it's acceptable to ask about it. Under normal circumstances, Ross would just ask question after question about how the eye had been lost. Something along the lines of, "Did it hurt? What were you doing? Did you call for help? You know you don't look so good? That fake eye makes you look weird." Ross agreed not to question our friend about his eye.

When the friend and his girlfriend arrived, Ross looked at him but didn't say anything about his eye. Later that night, Ross asked, "Are the two of you married?"

Our friend replied, "No."

"Are you going to be married?"

"Well, we're not for sure."

"Well, it could be that eye she's worried about."

In December 2007, we were in an ice storm and lost electricity for almost a week. While we were concerned about heat and the essentials, all Ross cared about was how many minutes it would be until his TV came back on. When we said our prayers that night, he told his brother to make sure and don't forget to pray for the cable.

Ross: "Mom?"

Me: "Yes, Ross."

Ross: "You know, I heard on the radio that people are getting electricity rage."

Me: "Really?"

Ross: "I think I'm getting that."

Me: "Why do you think that?"

Ross: "Because ever since I woke up this morning, I've been on my dark side."

I recently took Ross and his younger brother, Rhett, to play racquetball. Ross seemed to be interested in the sport and since he avoids all other physical activity like the plague, I thought we would give it a try. About halfway through our hour of court rental time, Ross decided he wanted a drink. I told him I had brought water and that it was in the gym bag. He told me the water wasn't cold enough so he didn't want it. I then told him there was money in the bag and he could go and get a Gatorade out of the vending machine. He came back crying, saying the vending machine took his money and didn't work. I told him as soon as I finished, which would be in about 10 minutes, that I would get him a drink.

As we were leaving, Rhett thanked me for bringing them to play and said he had had a good time. Ross then became upset again. He said, "I didn't have as much fun as I thought I would have. I was thirsty and wanted a drink."

I said, "If you were that thirsty, you could have walked down and got a drink out of the water fountain."

"What!" he said. "I didn't know they had water fountains. Stupid, stupid me! Ugh, that makes me so mad!" To most people, this seems like a trivial issue—just go and get a drink. But for the Asperger's child, the old adage of making a mountain out of a molehill applies. The rigidity of their thought process seems to overrule any amount of logic you try to convey.

Ross's comments on his memory: "I don't know why I can't remember things. My brain just kicks it out. I can't get everything in my head like I want it to be. I like for things to fit right in that place in my mind."

Ross on the importance of his dog: "Jackie (our Shihtzu dog) is the most important to me besides family. My life would be ruined if Jackie died. I would never smile again."

Ross on breath: "I don't like the smell of breath. Not of anyone. Not even after they brush their teeth. I hold my breath as long as I can. I don't like people close to me."

Ross: "Mom?"

Me: "Yes, Ross."

Ross: "I like it when the wind blows."

Me: "You do, why is that?"

Ross: "Because the trees talk."

Ross's comments on my work schedule (I worked two jobs): "Why do you work two jobs? For Pete's sake, you are a working woman of madness."

Ross, on familiarity: "I like using the same things over and over. I like sitting in the same place. I don't feel comfortable sitting in another desk or place from where I sit."

Ross, on dressing for church: "I don't like church shirts...feel too fancy."

Age 13:

Ross's explanation of how it feels for someone with OCD to be stuck on a thought: "I can't help it. It's like bobbing itself out—like the biggest star in the sky."

One day Ross asked me a question, to which I gave him my honest answer. He said, "Thanks, Mom," in a sarcastic voice, to which I replied, "You asked me to tell you the truth." Ross said, "No, I meant, I wanted the positive truth!"

One day Ross was disrespectful to me. I called him on his behavior. His reply was, "I'm sorry. I'm nothing better than a two-faced jackal."

Ross had to complete a project for school in which he had to read a book about a character and do a book report. In the report, he was asked to pick out ten key items in the story and answer the following question: "If you could meet your character today, do you think you would be friends? Why or why not?"

This was Ross's response:

The reason I think Abraham Lincoln and I would get along is because we're both smart. We also love to read. The book says that he read a book every chance he had. I love to read non-fiction books with lots of good pictures and a lot of information and data.

We're both kind and gentle natured. Although I have the tendency to be a little self-centered, I have a great heart and I love my family members, friends, God, and Jesus.

We both had obstacles to overcome when we were children. For instance, when I was a child, I had only two friends, and he had a family death crisis to overcome. But look at us now. I have a lot of outstanding friends and Lincoln became the president.

We're both interested in the government and other people. We also like to help others in need. As president, he influenced many people and I intend to help a lot of people when I grow up too.

Ross had a recurring episode with the flu, which included diarrhea, which he absolutely hates. After about three trips to the restroom, he turned to me and said, "I'm not going to take this anymore." Later on that day, he told me how bad his bottom was hurting. I responded with, "Bless your heart." He said, "No Mom, it's not my heart that hurts, it's my bottom."

Ross had a severe fear of wasps. One day there was a wasp near us and I killed it. Ross said,"Are you sure you killed it? Are you sure you pierced the exoskeleton?"

Ross told me recently that if he ever had to move away from me, that he would starve. I asked what he meant. He said, "I get scared of the dark and it paralyzes me. I'm afraid I would never leave my room and be able to walk to the kitchen in the dark. It doesn't even have to be dark inside. If the sun is down, there is no safe territory."

Ross on "getting stuck": "When I get stuck and I really want to do something and I can't, it's like a blood sucking leech glued to my head—no, hot glued to my head...it's painful. It's like friction on top of my brain when I want something. It's like pushing down right on top of my head."

Ross: "Mom?"

Me: "Yes, Ross."

Ross: "Look at the sun. It's like a mystical orb hovering in the sky."

In the Spring of 2010, when Ross was 14, we had to make a trip to the doctor. Ross was sick and we thought he had strep throat. I have a hard time convincing him to go to the doctor because of his fear of shots. He made me promise, triple swear, and then promise again that he would only get a shot if it was a life or death situation. Once we got to the doctor's office, there were masks available on the counter if someone had a fear of germs or spreading germs. Of course, we both wore one at Ross's request.

When the doctor took a look at Ross's throat, she said we needed to test for strep. This involved swabbing the back of his throat. Now, based on what has been discussed in this book, exactly how easy do you think it's going to be to stick a Q-tip on Ross's tonsil?

You are exactly right! First he was trying to convince the nurse that he could cough in his hand, and they could test the bacteria in his hand. When that didn't work, he said he thought he would throw up. So here I was, holding a trashcan up to Ross's mouth, trying to convince him that this is the only way for them to get what they need for the strep test. Every time he would open his mouth and stick his tongue out, the very minute the nurse got the Q-tip in his mouth, down went his jaw muscles. This image is quite amusing if you're reading about it in a book, but if you're living this moment, it's not so funny!

Ross: "The stupid curiosity of the cat did get it killed."

Ross: "Even when you think you have me figured out, you still haven't."

One day school was cancelled because of inclement weather. On this day, the wind was blowing hard. Ross commented, "Beefiness does have its advantages."

Ross had another school day that was cancelled because of bad weather. We had already left the house for school when we heard about the cancellation so Ross asked if we could go to McDonald's. As we entered the parking lot, he started talking about the smell of McDonald's and how good the smell was. As we pulled up to the drive-through window, he said, "Wow, I'm getting a little too pumped up over a cinnamon melt."

CHAPTER FIFTEEN

Family Sentiments

Raising a child with special needs affects everyone in the family. Here are the insights of two other members of the family who have loved Ross and persevered with him through the years.

My First Grandchild
(Judy Little, Ross's Grandma)

Ross was my first grandchild. Dee had some trouble with the pregnancy and we prayed fervently for this child. My, what a blessing he has been. I was the first one to hold Ross because they took Dee for some minor surgery after he was born. Ross was a fussy baby and we just thought he had colic. He was inconsolable and nursing him seemed the only way to calm him down. Dee had very little sleep during those early days and we had no clue as to what was ahead.

As Ross became older, he would line up all his animals in a row and if one was ever switched, he would notice it immediately. He became obsessed with dinosaurs. He knew every kind, how much they weighed, and what they ate. He has drawn some very excellent pictures of them. He has a photographic memory and can draw something he has seen on television.

Ross has always loved to come to our house in the summer. Since he had separation anxiety when he was away from his mother, we felt honored that he felt comfortable with us. He has always been close to his Pepaw, Lonnie, my husband. Lonnie would get in the floor and play with Ross for hours. The last time we visited, Ross said, "Pepaw, I love you." Dee said that doesn't happen very often.

When Ross was about seven, he asked my mom, "What are those lines on your face?" She said that when you get older, you get wrinkles. He said, "How old are you anyway?" Ross has trouble knowing what could hurt someone's feelings. He is just brutally honest.

Nothing is ever easy with Ross, but now that we better understand his disability, it is easier to cope with. I met Dee and Ross in Dallas and took him to Dr. Clements. He had to be off of his medications for several days so they could test his brain. In the motel room, he would run and jump on the bed then he would get in the swivel chair and go round and round. He was jumping off the sofa when the phone rang and the front desk said the people under us were complaining about the noise. He was out of control. The next day at the doctor's office, he was sitting backward in the chair, banging his head on the wall! Some people have been critical of the decision to put Ross on medicine, but I think the medication has been a God-send.

At Dr. Clements' office, they had to put in an IV so the medicine would show what was going on in Ross's brain. What an ordeal! Like I said, nothing is ever easy with Ross. Now I don't mean to paint a bleak picture. Ross is unique and wonderful. He has kept Dee and I laughing at the funny things he says. Like the time when Dee and Ross were at the cosmetics counter and the sales lady said to Ross, "You are so handsome, would you like to be my boyfriend?" He looked at her and said, "You do realize there is an age difference here!"

I do want to applaud my daughter. She has been very proactive in finding help for Ross. She has read countless books and taken him to the best doctors she could find. She has been so patient and loving to Ross. He thinks the sun and moon rise just for her. Ross is extremely intelligent and I think his dream of saving the world will come true.

Sibling Rivalry
(Rhett Phillips, Ross's 10-year-old brother)

Being Ross's brother is hard. He is frustrating and expects me to do things for him. He won't look for things on his own. I have to be the flexible one. I review his countless drawings and play the games he wants to play. But when it's my turn to play a game I want, he says he is too tired. He wants people to do things for him, but he's not so good at giving back to others. He talks a lot. He goes on and on about a topic. Sometimes it's hard to get my turn to talk. I feel like Ross gets attention because he is more difficult. He makes me so mad sometimes. I just want him to be fair.

Although he is difficult, I love him a ton. I love him. I love him. I love him. I enjoy hanging around him. I appreciate his efforts to do stuff. I like it when he wrestles with me. I have liked it for as long as I can remember. Mom has pictures of us wrestling when I was real little. He can be generous. He gave me a cell phone. He will give me money if he has it, to buy whatever I want.

I have learned a lot about science and animals, like dinosaurs, Big Foot and The Loch Ness Monster. Ross knows so much about that stuff. It is hard for me to deal with him when he is not reasonable. I have learned to be more patient. I will stand up for kids that are being bullied. I have learned to eat the food while it's there, cause Ross will suck it up like a vacuum.

My mom helps me out with Ross. She gives me a lot of attention and snuggles with me when we watch football and our favorite movies. She is always there for me when I need her. She will take time for me. I like little things she does for me the most. I like it when all of our family does things together. It's the smallest things I like the best.

🌀

If you suspect your child has a disorder, the following is a list of items that can assist you in confirming your suspicions and following through on getting your child the help they need. I often wondered why someone didn't give me a list that said, "If you have a child with Asperger's or ADHD, do the following...." I searched for information and found valuable tools in different information and books, but I often wondered why someone hadn't developed something comprehensive.

Not all items on this checklist will be relevant to all children. My goal is to provide you with a list of items to investigate to determine the items that best suit your situation. I've often felt like a turtle in the road, laying on my back and struggling with all my might to turn over and find the right path. I will say this sternly—*you are the best advocate for your child.* No one wants the best for your child more than you do. There isn't going to be anyone who will pay attention to the details like you will. When you have a child with a special need, that is exactly what it is—a special need. Many teachers and educators have limited knowledge, at best, concerning the challenges your child faces. You have to be the one who interfaces for your child. Some may label this as the "squeaky wheel syndrome," in other words, the one who makes the most noise is the one who gets the attention. It must be clear to educators, doctors, therapists, counselors, and everyone else involved that you are interested in your child's success and that you are holding them accountable for their part.

1. See a Developmental Pediatrician.

2. Consult an Occupational Therapist to help identify sensory issues.

3. Consult an allergist.

4. Consider physical therapy.

5. Enlist the assistance of a Speech Pathologist.

6. Consider securing a SPECT Scan.

7. Ask your doctor about supplements such as Omega 3.

8. Research, research, research. Remember, knowledge is power.

9. Determine if your child qualifies for an IEP (Individual Education Program). For more information, visit http://idea.ed.gov.

10. Develop a relationship with your child's school counselor.

11. Meet with your child's teachers and develop relationships.

12. Educate your child's teachers on the best methods to use with your child.

13. Determine if your child qualifies for classroom support.

14. Research schools that specialize in serving kids with Asperger's Syndrome and ADHD.

15. Explore Music Therapy.

16. Encourage exercise.

17. Pay attention to your child's diet and nutrition.

18. Join a Social Skills Group.

19. Lava Lamps, weighted blankets, and swings can be very soothing.

20. Consider brushing and massage therapy.

21. Formulate your own list of calming procedures before bed.

22. Give your child positive reinforcement.

23. Formulate written routines.

24. Remove clutter from your home to maintain organization.

25. Learn to prepare your child for upcoming situations.

26. Surround yourself with positive affirmations.

27. Pick your battles.

28. Learn to relax.

29. Find humor in everyday life.

30. Look for the brilliant characteristics of your child.

31. Provide unconditional love.

32. Set boundaries and let your child know what you expect.

33. Remember that God has given this child to you for a reason. Seize the opportunity.

William Ross Phillips's Birthday Condition Wish List

There must be that white cake I love so much.

It must be at Mazzios.

We must invite all my class mates.

There must be balloons.

There must be all my presents at the party.

Everyone has to have a great time.

There must be 14 candles on the cake.

I also want Mazzios customers to sing me the happy birthday song.

Ross created this list for me in preparation
for celebrating his 14th birthday.

Ross and Rhett Phillips. June 2011.
Courtesy of TG Photography. www.tgphotographybytrisha.com

Ross with his father, Phil Phillips.

Ross was obsessed with going to dig for diamonds
even though it was brutally hot. We succumbed to his wishes,
only to have him declare it was a "death trap."

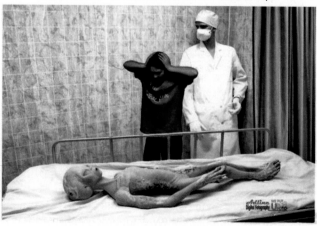

Ross has always had a fascination with aliens. This picture was
taken in 2007 in Roswell, NM at the International UFO Museum.

Dear President Obama,

I have a plan to see if there's life out in our universe. I
know I have the technology to do it. But I don't have the
money, but my plan I mentioned about earlier. My plan is a
way to make a lot of money for the program. I'm William
Ross Phillips. But everyone just calls me Ross. I'm thirteen
years old. I live in Owasso, Oklahoma in Timber Gate. My
address is 18894 East 80th St North. Here's my plan. First,
we'll set up funding programs. Since two thirds of the
world believes in aliens, we'll get enough money in a year
or two. Second, we'll build my design. Next, we'll check
for flaws in my design. Then, we'll fix my flaws in my
design. After that, we'll test my design. Finally, we'll shoot
into space and come back in a month or two. Send back a
letter and say if you accept my plan or not. If you accept, in
your letter, tell where we will discus my plan If you accept
my letter, I'll tell you a way to make pure energy with no
waste deposits. A.K.A: A way to make pure energy with no
waste. I'll trough in that information for free, If you accept
my letter.

By William Ross Phillips

This letter is a great example of the way Ross's mind works.
Ross assumes everyone is as fascinated with aliens as he is.

All that my mom does that I'm thankful for

: = I'm thankful...

: that my mom is there every day to protect me.

: that she puts up with me for most of her life.

: that my mom has the largest heart, besides God and Jesus.

: that my mom makes me food for my hungry belly.

: that she loves me.

: that she is there when I need her the most, and when I just need something small.

: that she pays attention to me.

: that she makes me sweets.

: that she will be there for a long time.

: that she is beautiful and cute.

: that she also teaches me about Christianity.

William Ross Phillips

Ross gave this to me for Mother's Day this year.
This was one of my best gifts ever!

The Light Paradox   *2-13-11*   *By William Ross Phillips*

Mass is how big an object is in relationship to its **Weight**. So, that means, in simpler terms, that the larger an object, the bigger it's **Mass**. **Density** involves some. That means **Light** shouldn't exist, because, it's **Massless**. Is **Light** a **Paradox**?

A **Paradox** is an apparent contradiction in physical descriptions of the **Universe**. in other words, if you went back in time, in a time machine, and killed your grandfather; how could have you been born, and therefore, traveled back in time to kill him? The time machine just wouldn't work. The **Universe** just finds ways to prevents **Paradoxes**, every time. Then again, maybe not.

What if **Light's a Paradox**? If it was a **Paradox**, which being **Massless** should make you a **Paradox**, then why does **Light** exist? Does this mean that **Paradoxes** can exist, thus proving the **Multiverse Theory**? Probably. Here below is the new science info on the **Universe**.

- Light is a Paradox
- The Multiverse Theory should be true

Ross is regularly forming theories and attempts to explain them to me. I listen, although I'm embarrassed to say, it really doesn't register.

Courtesy of TG Photography. www.tgphotographybytrisha.com

ABOUT THE AUTHOR

In addition to being a mom to her two sons, Dee Phillips-Goodnight teaches high school at Tulsa's East Central High School, where she is passionate about educating her students. She also sells Real Estate for Chinowth and Cohen Realtors.

Dee knows that it is only through the strength of Christ that she has the ability to do what she does. She has a compassionate and caring spirit that is a direct result of the adversity she has faced in life.

Ross continues to go to school at Town and Country School in Tulsa. He hopes to graduate and go to college to study aerospace engineering. He says he will never give up on his dream to "Save the World." He has a deep desire to contribute to making the world a better place. Every day is a challenge for him, but he is diligent in his efforts. He hopes to someday be able to help other children who face the same struggles he faces.

www.mysilentscream.org